TOWARD A MINOR ARCHITECTURE

THE MIT PRESS

Cambridge, Massachusetts

London, England

TOWARD A MINOR ARCHITECTURE

JILL STONER

MIT Press books may be purchased at special quantity discounts for business or sales promotional use. For information, please email special_sales@mitpress.mit.edu.

This book was set in Adobe Garamond Pro by the MIT Press. Printed and bound in the United States of America.

Library of Congress Cataloging-in-Publication Data

Stoner, Jill.
  Toward a minor architecture / Jill Stoner.
      p. cm.
  Includes bibliographical references and index.
  ISBN 978-0-262-51764-5 (paperbook : alk. paper)
1. Architecture and society. 2. Architecture, Modern—21st century—Philosophy. I. Title.
NA2543.S6S783 2012
720.1′03—dc23

                                                          2011030773

For my students

CONTENTS

> But how strange the change
> From major to minor.
> —Cole Porter, "Ev'ry Time We Say Goodbye"

Like most of us, I dream spaces that seem impossible. In dreams we follow paths that would send Euclid spinning, enter territories ordinarily forbidden to mortals. William Gass once wrote that we should "dream beyond the bricks,"[1] but I think now, with so many bricks in place, that it is necessary to dream our way through them. When as architects we make the strange shift from major to minor, we acknowledge that there is no longer a beyond; *there* is only *here*.

At least in part, this book took shape as a way of decoding my own architectural projects, of which a colleague once remarked: "They feel as though no architect has been there." It took me years to unravel this dubious acknowledgment. I tend to design in response to forces not easily expressed through form. For me contemporary poems and stories often reveal these forces; our metropolitan landscape of regretful constructions provokes them. My preference for working within existing buildings with all their hierarchies of power and unforeseen conditions in place, and my attraction to the particular assemblages of corporate culture, reflect a particular kind of optimism about our urban futures. I hope that this book offers multiple exits toward a more politicized practice of architecture.

Books of contemporary criticism are not really written; they are only composed. Images from the field and fragments from fiction are the pieces that form this particular narrative. But it is a story that could be told through infinite compositions of references and sources;

it claims no particular or final authority. My travels are not so considerable; I have seen only the places that I saw. My library is limited; I have read only the books that I read. I take enormous pleasure in orchestrating dialogues among writers who may never before have occupied the same page. These conversations are at the heart of what follows; and the epigraphs that divide each chapter into sections can be read as a subtext with its own dramatic structure.

But my debt is not only to the authors directly present in these pages; a multiplicity of institutions and individuals offered their encouragement and contributions along the way. I am grateful to the Graham Foundation for early support in the form of a research grant. At the University of California, Berkeley, students in my "Literature of Space" seminar have investigated the complex spaces of twentieth-century short fiction, and made many drawings of Neddy Merrill's swim. In graduate design studios I have been blessed with students who willingly suspend their disdain for office parks and corporate towers, and aggressively test subtractive strategies within such sites all around the San Francisco Bay. At the MIT Press, Roger Conover took a leap of faith, and directed me to *Socrates' Ancestor*,[2] his commitment solidified my own commitment to this project. Also at the Press, I am fortunate to have worked with Matthew Abbate and Erin Hasley; their talents, patience, and willingness have made the final stage of this process a genuine pleasure.

At various earlier stages, Erica Lee, Larry Bowman, Susi Stadler, Greig Crysler, and Greg Castillo read chapter drafts and gave insightful criticism. Eduardo Pindos, Ibone Santiago, and Sarah Stoner-Duncan helped with screen captures. Hsueh Han Lu was both my student and my teacher. He brought light to the section on blindness, and helped me to bridge the apparent chasm between the spaces of totalitarian regimes and those of contemporary America. David Buege has been my friend, colleague, provocateur, and English teacher for over twenty-five years. He introduced me to Corviale and the Torre de David, and reintroduced me to the infinite pleasures of

Moby Dick. His editorial exactitude and personal encouragement have been consistently present throughout this project, and his contribution cannot be overstated.

Mine is not the first call to architects to consider the potential for a minor architecture. In 1993, Yale University Press published Jennifer Bloomer's book *Architecture and the Text: The (S)crypts of Joyce and Piranesi*, in which she proposes "a revolutionary architectural criticism, a 'criticism from within' that goes deeply into the within, into the conventions of architecture's collusion with mechanisms of power."[3] I met Jennifer only a few years ago; we discovered immediately that our intellectual journeys and passions have an astonishing congruence. Had circumstances been different, we might have written this book together. As it is, I express my debt and affection, and gratitude for those snowed-in days at her mountain cabin in northern Georgia, where we talked our way through the night and toward a minor architecture.

San Francisco, October 2011

WHAT IS A MINOR ARCHITECTURE?

> To hate all languages of masters.
> —Gilles Deleuze and Félix Guattari, *Kafka*

> And herein are indirectly comprised many minor
> contingencies.
> —Herman Melville, *Moby Dick*

Where (in the world) is architecture going? As much as any art, it relies on *languages of masters* for momentum. In former times, its masters were deities and monarchs; since the industrial revolution, these have been replaced by the more abstract economic forces of "free" markets. Architecture's recent agendas have set their shallow roots in the soils of techno-virtuosity and eco-ethics. Yet still the discipline perpetuates the syntax of interior and exterior space, the production of buildings, and the architect's heroic aspirations. In thrall to influences and desires of corporate power, the major language of architecture is yet one more product of a culture increasingly dominated by symbolic capital. Its conventions teeter at the precipice of saturation, leading us to this seemingly strange proposition: Architecture can no longer limit itself to the aesthetic pursuit of making buildings; it must now commit to a politics of selectively taking them apart.

Political and economic powers set forth conditions of complicity in which major architectures are made.[1] But once made, buildings can be challenged to relinquish their share in this complicity. Though appearing to reside comfortably within the language of the majority, buildings may provide a medium within which a *minor* architecture might be situated. In this context, a minor architecture will operate both upon architecture's grammatical constructions of (virtual) power and within its physical, material form. Thus might an ornate theater be transformed into a utilitarian parking garage, or a half-finished corporate tower be taken hostage as a vertical *favela*.[2] In these and other instances, powerful forces arise in response to vacancy—not just in the form of empty rooms adapted for reuse, but through an encoding of these vacant spaces, and a subversion of major architecture's prevailing myths.

As we begin to investigate what minor architecture might mean, we must be prepared for its precise nature to elude capture. It rejects a definite article, divides and branches toward multiplicity.[3] So let us shift to the plural. In their deceptively simple spatial strategies and in their many guises as intensely complex theoretical constructions, minor architectures will alter and dematerialize the constructed world. They will be necessarily ephemeral, slip through cracks of Euclidean convention, and pay no heed to the idea of the formal. Form will tend to dissipate; material will give way to immaterial. Three dimensions may become two, then two become one: a line. The subtle aesthetic within these spaces will likely evade even the trained eye of an architectural photographer, though a canny journalist may be able to track the intricate relations of its existence, which are wrapped up in time.

> A minor literature doesn't come from a minor language; it is
> rather that which a minority constructs within a major language.
> —Gilles Deleuze and Félix Guattari, *Kafka*

The notion of minor architecture presented here emerges in response to Deleuze and Guattari's critical writing on minor literature.[4] In their study of Franz Kafka, a Czech who wrote veiled critiques of pre-Nazi Austria in the German language, they locate "minor" and "minority" as conditions that exist at the bottoms of power structures, yet hold an extraordinary potential for power. Emerging from within a major language, minor literature is that language intentionally impoverished, fractional, stripped of decoration and even of grammar.[5] In their analysis of Kafka's writing, Deleuze and Guattari slip fluidly between literary metaphor and descriptions of actual space. At one moment they identify the feminine characters in *The Trial* as "blocks," then describe and even diagram the architectural blocks of the Gentleman's Inn in *The Castle*.[6] Though writing about literature, they build a bridge between literature and architecture through the very words they use to describe Kafkan space. Blocks, segments, strata, connectors, rhizomes, planes of immanence, lines of flight—all of these describe spatial strategies and spatial effects. I borrow these terms to construct an argument for minor architecture from within the lexicon of minor literature. This is the minor squared. And like the square of any fraction, its quantitative value will continue to diminish. So while minor literatures still keep their authors in plain sight, minor architectures may tend to obscure their architects from view.

Deleuze and Guattari further define minor literature by these three characteristics: deterritorialization (and the implied reterritorialization), politicization, and collective enunciation.[7] In architecture as in literature, these traits exist in multiplicities, as both figurative and literal mechanisms, as both acts and consequences. But such multiplicities are deceptively light; they do not produce an excess. Instead, minor architectures perpetuate conditions of *lack*. More absence than substance, their spaces (like those of minor literature) are knowingly impoverished.[8] In its minor mode, the language of architecture is reduced to primitive elements, active verbs operating on concrete nouns. At the same time, redundancies proliferate in the form of repetitions (elemental) and vibrations (visual). These contribute to reframing familiar territory, to making the familiar strange. Estrangement is not conventionally nomadic; rather, it takes place largely in situ, as existing buildings and constructions respond to desires for escape, for blurred boundaries, and for collective expression. The stripping away of excess may be literal, as minor architectures employ subtractive mechanisms that dismantle the overwrought, manufactured, "meaningful" objects of culture through political force.[9]

But the political is slippery, Janus-faced. Politics can be a euphemism for the State[10] and its preoccupation with becoming sovereign; or it can refer to our more terrestrial daily life and its disparities.[11] Politics can conceal its agendas within the codes of abstract ideology (in parallel with religion); it can be summoned as a weapon of control, or wielded as a liberating force. All this is to say that politics can operate (spatially) either from the top of a power structure or from the bottom; the former produces major architectures out of which minorities can emerge. A *minor* architecture is political because it is mobilized from below, from substrata that may not even register in the sanctioned operations of the profession.

Political space engages the dimension of time, variously by its categorical divisions or by its liberating flow. Space politicized from above divides time into frozen segments. The architecture of the prison, for example, stratifies the mechanized agenda of incarceration; it operates through religious adherence to temporal laws of segmentation (the daily schedule) and permanence (the incommutable sentence). Similarly, the workplace refers to a particular space of control—a time line that daily reflects a repeating set of social and spatial relations. Workplaces are configured to maintain stability (a euphemism for obedience), production efficiency, division of labor, and alienation of laborers from their space of production. From the smallest office cubicle to the crossing patterns of merchant vessels, the flow of time is subordinated to time's economic value. The clock in the back of the house measures increments of lived control—"clocking in" is a polite term for getting to work. This manifestation of the political is a space where fluid time is expelled because it is threatening to power. The segmentation of time within a politically structured workplace obliterates the eternal and nonhierarchical relation between people and nature—substituting management of a false, measurable time (the eternity of work, the Situationists' "dead time")[12] for the perceived instability of fluid time.

And so (in the other instance) to consider a political space that *liberates from below* is to smooth, collapse, or expel the stratified mechanizations of lived time. Here emerges the sense of the political with which minor architectures are concerned. As conflict rises up, it reformulates collapsed time back into an undifferentiated stream. Fluid time (and its attendant space) surrounds and overwhelms the management of lived time; it is a contestation to management. An inmate damned to formal confinement, for two years or twenty, can certainly measure his cell and count the days as they pass; but those prisoners who appear throughout this book choose not to do so. With architecture's hard matter as a subversive ally, they find ways and means to escape the laws of both spatial and temporal segmentation.

As early as 1929, Georges Bataille wrote about the architecture of the majority in terms of its coercive powers, and its concurrent disenfranchisement and intimidation of those without power.[13] Bataille's point has been more or less obvious and relevant, depending on prevailing cultural conditions; architecture's excessive force escalates in tandem with an aggressive escalation of political authority. In the middle of the twentieth century, explicitly authoritarian buildings and spaces emerged out of totalitarian regimes, most visibly in Hitler's Germany and in the USSR after Stalin.[14] In the decades since World War II, corporate hierarchies have also reproduced themselves as architectural expressions of power. Though perhaps seeming less intimidating, these commissions are no less disenfranchising. They and their obedient offspring have so consumed our contemporary landscape that today Bataille's point strikes even truer. A half-century of architectural excess (played out through too much building with too little thought and too much ambition) has left us with a detritus of constructed objects that might serve as raw material for minor architectures politicized from below.

A familiar line from Bataille, "Architecture is the expression of the very soul of societies, just as human physiognomy is the expression of individuals' souls," is often misunderstood when taken out of its original context. For Bataille goes on:

> [But] only the ideal being of society, the one that issues orders and interdictions with authority, is expressed in architectural compositions in the strict sense of the word. . . . Thus great monuments rise up like levees, opposing the logic of majesty and authority to any confusion: Church and State in the form of cathedrals and palaces speak to the multitudes, or silence them. It is obvious that monuments inspire social good behavior in societies and often real fear. The storming of the Bastille is symbolic of this state of affairs: it is hard to explain this mass movement other than through people's animosity (animus) against the monuments that are its real masters.[15]

Opportunities for minor architectures emerge when the soul of a society is understood as more than a singularity, when—though a major soul constructs—minor souls await opportunities to de(con)struct. Minor architectures are, in fact, opportunistic events in response to latent but powerful desires to undo structures of power; and as such, minor architectures are precisely (if perversely) concerned with the privilege and circumstances of major architecture, the architecture of State and economic authority. Here it is useful to introduce Deleuze and Guattari's concept of striated and smooth space. Striated space is the sedentary, segmented space of the State, with its codes, logical orders, piecemeal differences, identities, and laws. Smooth space is non-Euclidean space, "a field without conduits or channels."[16] Striated and smooth form a dialectical pair; one would not exist without the other. And yet the distinction between the two is not like night and day. The space between them is immeasurable; they are a mixture with blurring, slippage, and overlap. Power triumphs by constructing striations. A desire to subvert the power of these constructions is a smoothing force. Minor architectures operate in that mercurial, indeterminate state that is the passage from striated to smooth, from closed system to open space.[17]

> He was forced instead to make his way through numerous
> little rooms, along continually curving passages and down
> tiny flights of stairs, one after the other, and then through
> an empty room with an abandoned desk in it until,
> eventually, only ever having gone this way once or twice
> previously, and then in the company of others, he found
> that he was totally and utterly lost.
> —Franz Kafka, *Amerika*

Though Kafka's novels and stories contradict and escape prevailing literary paradigms in ways made clear by Deleuze and Guattari, the architectural structures within his fiction are coercive, claustrophobic, labyrinths of relentless interiority (*The Trial*) and authoritarian object/subject constructions (*The Castle*/Klamm). This inescapable world, at first glance so remote from any "real" world, so seemingly isolated within an Escher-like geometry of self-conforming and self-referential relationships, mirrored the rise of new social and economic structures in the first half of the twentieth century. More precisely, Kafka possessed an uncanny ability to recognize the spaces of bureaucratic and authoritarian regimes before they had fully emerged. This was his genius, and one of the reasons he became an increasingly important figure as the cultural and political conditions of the twentieth century unfolded. His universe is a hermetic construct, a purely architectonic landscape. In his stories and novels, hierarchical spaces of industrial production and fiduciary management are brought under the roof of a singular narrative edifice within which there is no line of flight, no escape, not even any true arrival.[18]

Embedded in *The Trial* is a short (and also separately published) parable, "Before the Law." A supplicant seeking admittance to the Law is held at a threshold indefinitely by the authority of a doorkeeper who claims: "I am powerful. And I am only the least of the doorkeepers. From hall to hall there is one doorkeeper after another, each more powerful than the last. The third doorkeeper is already so terrible that even I cannot bear to look at him." His arguments are so intimidating that the protagonist "decides that it is better to wait until he gets permission to enter. . . . There he sits for days and years."[19] Within this parable is evidence of three myths that have dominated the major Western canons of architectural production. The first is the *interior myth*, a perception that an interior space (the space of the Law) lies beyond the gate and the gatekeeper. The supplicant is outside, waiting to be allowed in. But he is also *inside*, waiting to be let out; he is imprisoned within the system of belief that tells him the significance of the gate. The second is the *object myth*, embodied by Law as an object beyond the gate. The law/object is the central paradigm of *The Trial*, as it is of many of Kafka's stories. It appears solid and impermeable, and hovers with ever-ominous significance over all characters and all actions. The third is the *subject myth* in the person of the gatekeeper, whose horrifying face is potentially rendered almost amiable by the specter of an even more horrible gatekeeper that looms beyond the next gate, and so on, and on. But the supplicant cannot disbelieve the gatekeeper's powerful presence; he is paralyzed by the perceived authority, as though the gatekeeper himself were the architect of the law/object and sovereign over its interior.

These mythologies apply variously to all three of Kafka's novels. The setting of *The Trial* is an apparently generic city, though perhaps one with a non-Euclidean geometry. Its interiority is so absolute that to head in opposite directions can bring two travelers to the same location. The site of *The Castle*, with its density of unreachable fortress and impenetrable bureaucracy, is more a mythic village. It has no interior; its solidity is inviolable. In *Amerika*, vast spaces stretch infinitely toward Oklahoma. Objects are far apart, but each individual object (like the Occidental Hotel) is complex, functional, and repetitive, generated through the commodity machine that has consumed the landscape of the North American continent. These three fictional sites prefigure three key spatial conditions of the twentieth century, each of which contains a latent opposite. The space of *The Castle* is a fascist machine, pressing bodies and documents together into a solidified obstacle to the Castle itself, which is the ultimate architectural object, symbolic and unattainable. *The Trial* constructs a seemingly more passive model of totalitarian space, keeping bodies apart through intimidation and miscommunication, rendering interiority absolute. *Amerika* reflects that new-world engine of territorial exploitation disguised as opportunity. Each of these sites has a corresponding architectural form; each site, each form, is characterized above all by segmentation.

Consider two pervasive hard segmentations in architectural discourse: the dichotomous private and public and the even more fundamental binary of nature and culture. Minor architectures can blur these boundaries, turning hard segments soft. Obviously domination and authority can flourish in private, but they do also (and more subversively) in public. Who is more public than a Guantánamo detainee, what more than the execution of Saddam Hussein, the crush of Katrina victims into the New Orleans Superdome, or the endless stream of reality television? Certainly the space of the *public* is, in these contexts, a euphemism for the space of the State; but in fact the State forms a wall between public and private. We cannot blithely argue (as various discourses of environmental design commonly do) that spaces earmarked as "public" and "cultural" necessarily produce spaces of democracy. Culture and nature deploy an equally powerful spatial currency; the State apparatus is an organized power that has insidiously built an illusory distinction between them. Rodents in our national parks are protected; rats in our cities are exterminated.

Power structures operate by fabricating such dichotomous distinctions: by stratifying, filing, sequencing, making categories and concordances, endlessly organizing. In Deleuzian terms, these all form blocks. The blocks leave gaps between them. (In the construction of the Great Wall of China, the strength of the wall lies not in its physical continuity but in the very myth and legend of its existence.)[20] Minor architectures may emerge either in the movement from one segment to another or as lines of force within the zones *between* segments. These forces are purposeful but unstable. They obliterate conventional geometries to bend and join with time. They reshape space by transforming it.

Lines of force may resist enclosure (interiority) and become lines of flight. They may reject image, weight, and solidity, causing volumes (objects) to shatter. The force of collective desire may displace some perceived authority (subject) from its central position of power. The constructions of culture may be repositioned as a primal (natural) landscape.

I am well aware that I have never written anything but fiction.
—Michel Foucault, *Power/Knowledge*

Kafka's fiction seems to contain apparent and latent conditions from within which minor spaces might emerge; yet they cannot do so, precisely because their architectonic structures are so inflexible. But in other regions of literature's universe, elements of minor architecture are already embedded (perhaps one could even say hidden) within larger narratives. Often such literary fragments are tangential to their author's intentions. The investigation of their spatiality is not within the discipline of literary criticism. Instead, literature provides the medium for an oblique but critical approach to architecture.

Let us introduce two images, each set in the 1970s and each from a work of fiction. The first: in an Argentine prison a journalist sits on her bed in a solitary cell, reading into the walls a mnemonic text through which she records her ordeal. The second: in New York's affluent Westchester County, a man reclines alongside a backyard pool, contemplating a swim home along a metaphorical river named for his wife. Embedded within these stories are examples of seemingly polar conditions of politicized space: imprisonment and territorial freedom. But each scene operates through a spatial paradox that is not readily apparent; each in fact is an enactment of its perceived opposite. Cecelia and Neddy (who reappear later in this book) are mere instruments of their stories' true and shared protagonist, which is space itself.

As Walter Benjamin read the elemental artifacts of nineteenth-century Paris as though they were texts,[21] so can we read elemental fragments of twentieth-century fiction as though they are architecture.

Fiction offers nonvisual images of space that the camera cannot reach, and temporal/spatial enactments that lie outside the conventions of architectural representation. The spatial conditions that appear within these narratives may seem tangential by-products of other forces; they sneak through cracks in the primary plot. In certain genres of modern literature,[22] space is particularly active. It replaces character (Robbe-Grillet), it becomes evocative (Proust), threatening (Poe), politicized (Orwell, Atwood), or animated (Borges). An unsung protagonist, space may be willful and present without or beyond its author's intentions. Here is the paradox of fiction as a source and measure of minor architectures: the medium that relies on discourse and metaphor yields, in those zones between strata, spaces that confront and even deny their metaphoric and territorial contexts. An absence of authorial intent allows literary sites their politicized, minor quality; this is also true for the architectural spaces within them. We might say that a work of minor architecture is architecture in its most literary mode.

So in the following chapters I call on classics and lesser-known works of twentieth-century fiction, locating fragments within which occur elements of minority or the explicit exclusion of minority. This then becomes a new narrative, one that transcends both plot and style, and forms a consistent plane upon which the potential for minor architectures in "our" world may become legible. The broad context of this literary landscape is like a vast archaeological site, but the retrieved fragments (like pottery shards in the ruin of a dwelling, or bones in a tomb) are small, perhaps seeming inconsequential. Each one is its own tactical line of force, and also a potential piece of a new assemblage. Though their lines may intersect, the fabric remains unfinished and inconclusive. Each line points toward where it may never arrive.

> The archdeacon gazed at the gigantic edifice for some time
> in silence, then extending his right hand, with a sigh,
> towards the printed book which lay open on the table, and
> his left towards Notre-Dame, and turning a sad glance
> from the book to the church,—"Alas," he said, "this will
> kill that."
> —Victor Hugo, *The Hunchback of Notre Dame*

Hugo's "this" is the ephemeral space of words within books; he warns that it may gain power and become more solid than those "books" of stone which we call buildings.[23] Some might argue that this has indeed come to pass, that first the printed book and now the proliferation of social and economic spaces produced through electronic media have rendered architecture impotent. Yet architecture still conveys a particular kind of spatial power. The modern condition of estrangement (or alienation) has become perversely palpable through buildings, the very material of which implies permanence, stability, and community. Particularly in the second half of the twentieth century, alienation associated with labor, and specifically the *division* of labor, was gradually subsumed by a different kind of alienation, tied more closely to geography than to history. This occurred at roughly the same time that the division of labor turned from blue-collar to white-collar work, from a Fordist (state-capitalist) economy to one of (neoliberal) flexible accumulation.[24] In the decades following World War II, this shift (e.g., from the making of a car to the selling of a car) produced a body of architectural work that is now almost universally acknowledged as both strange and estranging. What is it that makes this dominant paradigm seem strange, when it so carefully adheres to the grammars of architecture's current official language? Perhaps in order to engage minor architecture as a practice, we must first propose the axiom that *there can be no official language of architecture*.

For more than two millennia, we have endlessly debated the aesthetic vocabulary of buildings, their formal diagram, the means of their production, the efficiency of their function, and the nuances of their meaning. At the same time we have accepted nearly without argument the fundamental notion of their durability, which also means permanence. Marx's historical materialism, when made spatial, unmasks the myth of architectural permanence. His metaphoric description of the revolutions of 1848 as "small fractures and fissures in the dry crust of European society"[25] prophetically sets the stage onto which the premise for a minor architecture can enter. The buildings of the past fifty years are themselves such a dry crust, seemingly solid but primarily air. Their shells obtain the illusory images of obsolescent institutions. These days the edifice is frequently empty; yet still it conveys a weighty ambition that even high rates of vacancy cannot vanquish.

Space is pure act.
—Joseph Raphson

Walter Benjamin's *destructive character* "knows only one watchword: make room; only one activity, clearing away. His need for fresh air and open space is stronger than any hatred."[26] But turned toward a minoritarian agenda, the action that Benjamin calls *de*structive becomes *con*structive. The clearing away of material and the activity of making room are both experiments with space and experiences of space.[27] Minor architectures are acts of clearing. Each act yields an emergent, revolutionary space, even as that space begins to close in behind. It is space displaced, a *deterritorialization*. It challenges authority and its management of time; it is *political*. It overrides heroic aspirations with an inclusive, *collective voice*. The lines of force that generate minor architectures begin always in the middle, yet not from the center. They have only their elastic length, with never a true beginning or end. These lines are complex trajectories that open outward. Their calculus is more that of Leibniz than of Newton,[28] an approach to zero-degree space. A line of desire locates a weak point within a seemingly orthodox and stable form; it is a pry bar that forces open a crack of thin space that weaves into and intersects with other thinnesses. Minor architectures tend to proliferate; their thready multiplicity is highly unstable, variously generative, subtractive, and reactive.

If we invert Raphson's axiom to read, "Action is pure space," then we encounter architecture's back door. Yet there is no arrival; instead, this door is an exit toward uncertainty. It gives way to another door, and then another. Unlike in Kafka's parable, no gatekeeper guards this gate. Neither the law (object) nor the sovereign (subject) lies within, for there is no interior, only multiple thresholds that imply architecture's desiring state—to become exterior, to find an outside. Minor architectures operate from outside the major economy, potentially outside the architectural profession, and outside prevailing critical frameworks—outside these dominant cultural paradigms, but *inside* architecture's physical body. And from this inside, they establish *outside* as an oblique destination. A building's interior may truly shed its hard enclosure, like a reptile emerging from its obsolete skin. But transformations may also transcend this literal, material mode of escape; new spaces may disappear *into* the image of their major host. This is often a matter of economy, for minor architectures tend to rely on minor resources.

The spatial conditions we are calling minor may already be close by, latent within our consumer objects, veiled by property relations. To tease them out is to think outside conventional visual paradigms, to resist the linearity of time and the seduction of progress. The study of minor architectures is itself a study in architectural kinships—but not those derived from geographical responsiveness (regionalism), aesthetic canons (style), or program-driven institutions (typology). Instead, it uncovers a shared spatial code that transcends conventional categories, ensuring that minor architectures will always operate through complex multiplicities.

If, as Michel de Certeau suggests, "space is practiced place,"[29] these minor operations might be construed as *practiced space.* Through actions that are often small in scope but powerful in their effects, and in the absence of both behavioral and aesthetic agendas, minor architectures can seem simultaneously insignificant and subversively instrumental—possessing an alchemy that dissolves material, privileges air, inscribes meaning onto surfaces, folds exteriors inward and interiors outward, and blurs definitive objects into contingent relationships. The idealized modernist belief of physical determinism is turned on its head, revealing those conditions in which space can be the result of action rather than the cause of behavior.

Minor architectures operate through verbs, not as nouns. Provoked by desires for resistance, fragmentation, and opposition, they may be mobilized *within* buildings that are underutilized or diminished by real or perceived obsolescence. These sites of origin are not autonomous; rather, they are part of an enormous construct, an ur-urbanism that reaches beyond city limits to engage all that has been built "according to plan." Minor actions form assemblages of space; they disassemble binary oppositions of inside and outside, public and private, sanctioned and subversive, large and small. They reframe the definition of architecture from *the making of buildings with materials of nature* to *the making of spaces within the already built.* Such works may remain unrecognized, and they will likely leave some wreckage in their wake even as they challenge the perceived wreckage that precedes them. They will have consequences of incompleteness and imperfection; but minor architects delight in imperfect, incomplete outcomes.

At the end of his scathing critique of architecture's beholden state, Manfredo Tafuri refers to "impotent and ineffectual myths" that hold the profession hostage to the powers of capital.[30] It is now thirty years later, and these myths have gained even greater currency. Recurring conditions of crisis—foreclosure, bankruptcy, abandonment, poverty, environmental collapse, and corporate scandal—frame a physical landscape rife with multifarious forms of excess. Along the road to any airport in almost any city in the world, the buildings that crowd our view represent the certainty of a global

majority language: the language of profit. Most we deem ugly;[31] they provoke the disdain even of many within the profession that produced them, and that continues to do so. Vacancies are currently high; yet these buildings repel our desire, so we avert our gaze. Yet here in full force (though in radically different form) are the architectures of power that Bataille so precisely described seventy years ago. They place the argument for alternate and subversive spatial strategies squarely at our doorstep.

Our prevailing attitude to these chain hotels, office parks, discount stores, and planned developments reflects the professional elite's predilection for moral judgment. But if we suspend our judgment, these buildings can perversely provoke a spirit of play. To embrace this approach is to acknowledge architecture's relationship to its own characteristic law—that is, the law of space, or "space as law." At the same time, we can challenge and play with laws *outside* of space—the policies, codes, agreements, and approvals that are normal prerequisites for the practice of architecture. As with the buildings themselves, these perceived obstructions may open opportunities for minor but revolutionary architectural events.

Deleuze and Guattari refer to diabolical powers knocking at Kafka's door,[32] suggesting Kafka's prescient anticipation of three significant twentieth-century developments: Soviet Communism, National Socialism, and late capitalism. Each of these arose out of a highly ordered, determined system. Totalitarian space privileges interiority; it is passive, self-preserving, and frozen, with an agenda of subjugation. As a distinct kind of totalizing machine, Fascist space objectifies; it is active, destructive, and mobile, with an agenda of extermination. Neoliberal space is passive-aggressive, self-aggrandizing, and immaterial, with an agenda of profit. These spatial typologies map onto the interior, object, and subject myths that form the warp of this book.

We proceed from three assumptions: the interior takes flight, the object fractures, the subject dissolves. There are projects and tactics, experiments and statements that address all three. The chapters that follow do not remain territorialized within their rooms. Interior and object do not simply make a binary pair, nor do object and subject. The edges that appear to segment them from each other blur, thicken, and fuse into subtle indeterminacies. Vulnerable, permeable, and unstable, minor architectures appear only obliquely, within gaps formed and shadows cast by majority rule.

Poised now at the threshold of the interior, we turn to discover lines of escape that pass through seemingly solidified boundaries, provoking architecture to bend toward its own (minor) immanence.

THE MYTH OF THE INTERIOR

Hiding places there are innumerable, escape is only one,
but possibilities of escape, again, are as many as hiding places.
—Franz Kafka, *The Blue Octavo Notebooks*

Ask! How can the prisoner reach outside except by
thrusting through the wall?
—Herman Melville, *Moby Dick*

Architectural space need not only be bound to enclosure—finite, measurable, and palpable. It may also transcend material boundaries, flow maddeningly like mercury, soft-hard and fluid. Such space is found within texts both written and built. We find it in literature and in architecture; it flows teasingly among words and within walls, between interiors. Such quixotic space can be produced; it can return us in force to Kafka's innumerable possibilities of escape.

Words may weave a tectonic fabric, but every piece of architecture also constructs a text whose completeness is only apparent. Incompleteness generates imbalance, knocks against walls, shifts weight toward the outside. It is a desiring force, reactive to static powers of symmetry, hierarchy, and unforgiving containment. Within cities, buildings, and rooms (hidden inside our constructed narratives) are latent possibilities for exteriority that await both desire and opportunity. It is the expression of sovereign power that produces a desire for escape; it is the fabric of architecture, in all its material hardness, that provides the opportunity.

Interiors are the passive, self-referential and self-preserving spaces of sovereignty. And so our first image of a minor architecture is a *line of force* that redirects a thick vector of power into multiplicities of thin and thready flows. If architecture is an art, then its minor mode is an essentially politicized art of escape—challenging our fundamental understanding of container and of being contained. Containment is a relation without dynamism; it is historical, prefigured, assigned, remembered, and repeated. An interior is a segment separate from other segments and other interiors; it is from such static zones that minor architectures may emerge. Interior becomes exterior not simply by moving outside the norms and physics of architectural enclosure; its exit to the outside subverts the traditional interior/exterior dialectic of space through an assimilation of time.

Time is a critical accomplice to every act of escape. In fact, the idea of permanence can be understood as time's own interior, as time frozen or captured, as time's primal nature foiled. The act of escaping permanence is not a move toward a space without time, but rather an *exit* to time's exterior.[1] In this calculation, to escape is to reconfigure a relation to time—to undermine and overturn the authority of permanence and the self-preserving eternal. Western traditions of architecture have long been based on both the interiority of space (enclosure) and the interiority of time (permanence);[2] minor architectures release both space and time from their framed and familiar territories. Escape and duration merge into active lines of force that penetrate, blur, or even dissolve the distinguishing membranes which separate inside from out, and now from then.

What is Kafka's "indefinite postponement"[3] if not the enclosure of the present, the inability to mobilize the past or exit into the future?

"Couldn't we open the window?" asked K. ",No," replied
the painter. "It is only a sheet of glass let into the roof.
It can't be opened." . . . [K.] brought the flat of his hand
down on the feather bed and said in a feeble voice,
"That's both uncomfortable and unhealthy." "Oh no,"
said the painter, in defense of his window. "Because it's
hermetically sealed, it keeps the warmth in much better
than a double window, though it's only a simple pane
of glass. And if I want to air the place, which isn't really
necessary, for the air comes in everywhere through the
chinks, I can always open one of the doors or even both
of them."
—Franz Kafka, *The Trial*

Kafka is perhaps the consummate master of absolute interiority.[4] His
literary space has only elusive interiors, narratives that have no end,
no beginning, no real center, in fluid language that can barely be contained.[5] But the architectural spaces within his fiction are interiority
uncompromised. Particularly in the novels, doorways (but not windows) proliferate. Kafka's doors are always a way in, never a way out.
His strange and paradoxical geometries establish connectivity, but
without continuity. Interiors multiply relentlessly inward; they nest,
like the prose of Raymond Roussel, within an inviolable edifice of
enclosure.[6] Firmly they deny any possibility of escape.

In *The Trial* all rooms are stifling; everywhere is airlessness,
unventilated heat, and claustrophobia. Private rooms double as
offices or passageways; Josef K.'s own chamber opens into the bedroom of Fräulein Burstner, which becomes the strange first venue of
his ordeal. An inspector sits behind a desk that has been moved to the
middle of the room, three other men lurk in a shadowy corner, peer-
ing at framed photographs hanging on the wall. In the midst of this
bureaucratic setting "[a] white blouse dangled from the latch of the
open window."[7] Every scene is similarly crowded by suited men and

incongruous assemblages of objects, a commingling of officiousness and domesticity within rooms.

Directed to appear for his first formal interrogation at an obscure address in an outlying suburb, K. again encounters a set of domestic interiors that he must penetrate on his way to the Court of Inquiry. He navigates a series of apartments, each consisting of only one small chamber with a single window. On the fifth floor of the designated building, he enters one of these rooms. The tenant directs him through to another door: "K. felt as though he were entering a meeting hall. A crowd of the most variegated people—nobody troubled about the newcomer—filled a medium sized, two-windowed room, which just below the roof was surrounded by a gallery, also quite packed, where the people were able to stand only in a bent posture with their heads and backs knocking against the ceiling."[8] Some time later, while at his office at the bank, K. is visited by a manufacturer, who alludes to knowledge of his case and advises him to visit the painter Titorelli. K. at once leaves the bank and gives the address of the painter to a cab driver. He observes that he is heading in a direction exactly opposite to the suburb where his case is being tried and arrives in an "even poorer suburb"—perhaps a fitting image for the residence of a struggling painter. Upon entrance into the building he is accosted by a flock of young girls, who hang onto his coats and lead him up through the tenement staircases, along corridors, more staircases, more corridors, and up a final straight stair to an undistinguished wooden door at the top, on which is painted: *TITORELLI*. K. enters the painter's room, a hovel of plain boards crowded by a bedstead and dozens of canvases that cover the floor. (Many of the canvases are identical; Titorelli is a master of repetition.) Still, the girls' presence verges on omnipresence; they have remained at the top of the stair spying through the boards, they call out his every move even as K. attempts to focus the conversation on his case. The painter blocks and diverts the questions toward his own interests, yet K. cannot follow the thread. He lacks peripheral vision.

Again, an atmosphere of stifling domesticity. K. is encouraged to take off his jacket and to make himself comfortable on the bed; he is pushed down among the bedclothes. For some time, a second, half-hidden door escapes his notice. Eventually, the painter encourages him to leave by this means, and K. welcomes the chance to exit the room without having to run the gauntlet of young girls. As a seemingly obscure escape route, this proverbial back door is classically tantalizing. There is an awkward negotiation as K. climbs over the bed and trips over the paintings. He exits and is astonished! —the door leads not to some hidden staircase and thence to the anonymity of the street but instead into the very same courtrooms to which K. was directed immediately following his arrest. It is the same space; yet it cannot be the same space. Titorelli's suburb, presumably in the opposite direction from the court, appears to have doubled back on itself. The straight line and the loop have converged in a Euclidean paradox, once again preventing any possibility of escape.

As Walter Benjamin points out in an essay on Kafka, all of Kafka's doorways are theoretical obstacles. He compares their effect to Arthur Eddington's description of a mathematician attempting to cross a threshold:

> I am standing on the threshold about to enter a room. It is a complicated business. In the first place I must shove against an atmosphere pressing with a force of fourteen pounds on every square inch of my body. I must make sure of landing on a plank travelling at twenty miles a second around the sun—a fraction of a second too early or too late, the plank would be miles away. I must do this whilst hanging from a round planet, head outward into space, and with a wind of aether blowing at no one knows how many miles a second through every interstice of my body. The plank has no solidity of substance. To step on it is like stepping on a swarm of flies. Shall I not slip through? . . .
>
> Verily it is easier for a camel to pass through the eye of a needle than for a scientific man to pass through a door. And whether the door be barn door or church door it might be wiser that he should consent to be an ordinary man and walk in rather than wait till all the difficulties involved in a really scientific ingress are resolved.[9]

Like the threshold described here, Kafka's doors often stand open. Even so, they remain impassable. This is the state of mind—and the perpetual spatial consequence—that plagues Josef K. throughout *The Trial*. He may seem to move through the city, from one room to another, seeking the counsel of lawyers, businessmen, bankers, painters, and clergy—but he makes no progress whatever. Any potential discovery is effectively thwarted by and within the opaque interiors of the Law, which are in fact a single space without exit, congruent with the absolute interiority that characterizes K.'s life after his arrest.

Giorgio Agamben writes of life and law, "To show law in its non-relation to life and life in its non-relation to law means to open a space between them for human action."[10] In Kafka's universe, no such space seems to exist. Action is stifled by indolence. As we have seen in the parable of the supplicant at the gate, a man who seeks admittance to the Law is kept waiting his entire life. He is made an example, and he is on display.[11] He thinks he wants to go in, but in fact he is rooted (like Eddington's mathematician) at the threshold. The gate itself is open; the gatekeeper is the inhibition to its being crossed, a materialization (and personification) of impasse. And although the Law presumably lies unseen beyond the gate, its interiority is mythologized, sovereign, and powerful. The supplicant wishes admittance, but in fact it is another law, the law of interiority, that prevents his entering. He is actually *within* this law rather than *before* it. What lies beyond the gate is an outside that he will never reach.

Another short parable, "An Imperial Message,"[12] is embedded within the longer story "The Great Wall of China." A fleet-footed disciple visits the dying emperor at his bedside to receive a whispered message; his charge is to deliver it to a man in the remote country-side. In this tale Kafka has engendered a kind of Zeno's paradox in reverse;[13] as the messenger runs, the distance between him and his destination lengthens. An endless series of courtyards and staircases multiplies outward.[14] To pass through any of them is to gain nothing, for another set of redundant spaces lies beyond. Even in flight, the messenger is within the prison of this radiating geometry. Imprisoned at the other end is a man who sits by his window dreaming to himself, condemned to his own endless interior of frozen time (in)to which the message can never arrive.

I stood in the cell leaning against the cool iron door. I
took a step and was up against the wall. I went back again
to the middle of the cell, then to the left up to the wall,
I turned around, leaned against it heavily, it took only two
little steps to the cot at the opposite wall, I stood and
looked round: the floor grey-black, made of cement, the
door painted blue, an iron door, a window in one wall,
I called it the window wall, a bucket on the other wall, I
called it the bucket wall, the cot on the third wall, I
called it the cot wall, and above the cell door in a niche
a searchlight behind wire mesh. This was the cell: they
had assigned it to me, and I was busy taking possession
of it, taking possession of it.
—Horst Bienek, *The Cell*

Melville's epigraphic question at the beginning of this chapter may
seem rhetorical, but prisoners within literature (both fiction and
nonfiction) narrate events in which walls atomize and prison cells
change scale and size. The prisoner reaches an outside *without*
"thrusting through the wall." Escape modes include tapping, scratch-
ing, reading, writing, gazing, and pacing. Horst Bienek describes his
own escape obliquely, in the form of an appropriation, a stealing of
the self within the cell, a transcendence of both self *and* cell. Bienek
deterritorializes his cell by reconstructing it;[15] this he does by giving
names to things. His "line of flight" is admittedly semantic, an act of
nomination. Bienek exits the cell by taking possession of its space and
its contents; the possibility for escape resides in his ability to transform the space from *cell* to *room*.[16]

    Room may be understood as the most basic unit of architectural
interiority.[17] The first recorded use in English of the word *room* refers
to the cabin of a ship.[18] This small space below deck, which for our
purposes we might think subterranean, evokes Shakespeare's "cabin'd,
cribb'd, confin'd"[19]—an antithesis to open air. But *room* has an alternate etymological history that helps to explain its agency in

mechanisms of escape.[20] The original Indo-European root is thought to be *rew*, meaning "wide, open." The Latin *rus* means "open country" (hence, "rustic"), and the German verb *raumem* means "to vacate." To "make room" is to reestablish space as wide and open, to make space empty, to create vacancy. Bienek's "taking possession" is no more than a kind of *dispossession* of the space that has taken possession of him. The transformation from cell to room is from a space that already *is* (temporally closed, crepuscular) to one in a state of *becoming* (free, temporally open).

When Denis Hollier asks, "Is prison then the generic name designating all architectural production?,"[21] he is assuming and building upon Bataille's notion that (major) architectures operate with coercive force. Actual stories of imprisonment that narrate mechanisms of escape reflect the most basic principle of minor architectures: they operate precisely *within*, but in opposition to, the major language of their hosts. Consider the protagonist in John David Morley's novel *In the Labyrinth*. Like many political prisoners of totalitarian regimes, he is taken from his home in the night and given no indication of the nature of his offense. After many weeks in his solitary cell, and suffering from illness, he hears a sepulchral voice calling the name *Lazarus*. He thinks he is dreaming or perhaps languishing at some threshold between life and death. But when he hears the more banal sound of a human cough, he calls out:

"Who are you?"

"Ah, you can hear me at last. I've been trying to get you for some time. Feeling better?"

"Thank you. But where on earth are you?" I echoed in astonishment.

"Two cells down from you. Pleased to make your acquaintance at last. My name is Tibor Benjamin Lazar."

Lazar![22]

The disembodied voice of his neighbor below has been carried by a disused water pipe buried within the wall close to their beds. The wall *hides* the pipe, which in turn permits the very conversation the walls have been designed to prevent.[23] The pipe functions literally as a vertical, auditory line of flight, an invisible conduit *out* of solitary.

And there is this example of a line of flight that is horizontal, silent, and visible. The Argentine journalist Jacobo Timerman was also arrested in his home in the dead of night, and incarcerated for speaking out against the regime during Argentina's Dirty War.[24] Imprisoned for thirty months in solitary confinement, with no due process and frequent interrogations by torture, he describes a coincidence of space and time that engendered his own sublime moment of escape:

> Tonight, a guard, not following the rules, leaves the peephole ajar. I wait a while to see what will happen but it remains open. Standing on tiptoe, I peer out. There's a narrow corridor, and across from my cell I can see at least two other doors. Indeed, I have a full view of two doors. What a sensation of freedom! An entire universe added to my Time, that elongated time which hovers over me oppressively in the cell. Time, that dangerous enemy of man, when its existence, duration and eternity are virtually palpable.

Timerman's poetic reconstruction emphasizes the fragility of an event structure in which time and space conjoin. Once again, the very architecture designed to prevent escape paradoxically provides the mechanism through which escape can occur. Through the tiny peephole, Timerman simultaneously exits two interiors—that of the predictable and scheduled (time), and that of an isolating cell (space). He continues:

> The light in the corridor is strong. Momentarily blinded, I step back, then hungrily return. I try to fill myself with the

visible space. So long have I been deprived of a sense of distance and proportion that I feel suddenly unleashed. In order to look out, I must lean my face against the icy steel door. As the minutes pass, the cold becomes unbearable. My entire forehead is pressed against the steel and the cold makes my head ache. But it's been a long time—how long?—without a celebration of space. I press my ear against the door, yet hear not sound. I resume looking. *He* is doing the same.[25]

As power operates by enforcing spatial discontinuities, Timerman's narrative of that single night demonstrates how *resistance* to power can overcome the authority of those interior segments. The resistance comes necessarily from within; it links inside to inside, and by doing this it compromises the authority of the two separate cells. The guard is positioned as a functionary, attached to a sovereign state that rules by enforcing interiors. His job is to maintain separations. Thus, by leaving the peephole open, he becomes a spatial revolutionary—a minor architect. "Not following the rules," he abets an act of escape for Timerman and for the unnamed prisoner across the corridor.

Not space displaced by time, but time made spatial and given a proper name: "An entire universe added to my Time." Space extends time, and slows time down. Timerman's individual politics, his personal economy that is so radically tested through torture, exhaustion, hunger, and loneliness, is the very force of *lack* that compresses both time and space into spare but powerful infrastructures. The corridor takes on urban qualities (more a street than a road), a spatial connection between two private rooms across an in-between territory. This in-between becomes charged with unsanctioned sight—much like the courtyard in Alfred Hitchcock's film *Rear Window*.

Geometrically, the corridor is an effective material barrier by which to maintain and enforce the security of the block, and as a conduit to deliver food and to escort new prisoners to their cells. Across this seemingly linear space, Timerman's perpendicular gaze complicates the geometry, providing a cross grain that contradicts the hierarchical mechanisms of ordered incarceration. A particular kind of temporal emptiness, which is itself engendered through a guard's revolutionary act of omission, puts the meaning of the corridor into disequilibrium. Within this room (*open space, vacancy*) on that night, provoked by a reduction to the barest of human circumstances, an affirmation takes place. Timerman describes it even as a love affair, though he is not even sure if his lover is man or woman. "You blinked. I clearly recall you blinking. And that flutter of movement proved conclusively that I was not the last human survivor on earth in this universe of torturing custodians."[26] Through this minor event the corridor is both transgressed and possessed, both crossed and occupied. A new, lateral space violates the sovereign, axial one, and the peephole is transformed from a passive mechanism of surveillance into an active conduit that profanes the institutionalized, domesticated solitude. It becomes a tectonic force of escape, and bears out the Deleuzian axiom: "Sovereignty can only rule over what it is capable of interiorizing."[27]

Mr. Gorbachev, open this gate. Mr. Gorbachev, tear down this wall!
—Ronald Reagan, 1987

The Berlin Wall was first breached in November 1989, and in the early days of December those who could get their hands on a hammer and chisel converged to celebrate and participate in its physical destruction.[28] Within days, vertical gaps (what Paul Virilio calls "anorthoscopic slits")[29] opened up around the iron reinforcing bars embedded in the concrete. As with Timerman's peephole, these slots captured particular and fleeting views between an East and a West still separate enough to be powerfully joined. The slots were not only apertures for sight; hands reached through to make intimate contact between people (like Timerman and his fellow prisoner) who could not see each other clearly, had never before met, and might never meet again. These too were minor architectural events, the result of a passionate force *through*, producing lines of escape perpendicular to the line of the Wall. We can speculate, in retrospect, that the two Berlins had never been more intimately connected, even as their separate identities and interiors began to overlap, even as the separation between them began to dissolve.[30] By the summer of 1990 the Wall was literally gone; the space between the two Berlins, for such a short time thickened into a zone of exteriority, had disappeared into a new interior legislated by the laws of Western commerce and its bureaucratic servants of urban planning. The thirty-year history of a particularly ambiguous geography had come to an end.

In August of 1961, the Wall was decreed and its first phase executed in a matter of days, tracing lines mapped years before.[31] Even more than with most politically motivated constructions, the necessity for stealth and efficiency prevailed.[32] First came a wire fence, quickly unreeled across gaps between buildings, and then improved over the next several years. In 1965 the fence was replaced with an opaque wall of masonry blocks. At first, existing buildings were expediently assumed into its length, quickly effaced and defenestrated. This construction took more time, though in places the Wall rose quickly. In one moment during its construction, a photographer captured an elderly couple facing the half-built wall with their backs to the camera. They are being walled into exile. What fell within their sight, what remains in the photograph, was gone minutes later with the laying of the next tier of blocks. We see them at the moment just before an exterior denied to them became physically explicit.

For those within the wall and those without (who were actually within), the Wall embodied the paranoia, paradoxes, and contradictions inherent in Berlin's peculiar politics and compound geometry. As a barrier it functioned in multiple ways: physical deterrent, virtual intimidation, visible symbol of the Iron Curtain, provocation for improved technologies of escape. The German Democratic Republic officially named the wall the Anti-Fascist Protection Rampart, suggesting that Nazi sentiments might still exist in the West. But though publicly stated to be a barrier to keep Westerners out, its private agenda (and in history's hindsight its primary role) was to keep East Berliners and East Germans in.

Maps drawn between 1961 and 1989 reveal the relative interiority of the two Berlins as artfully ambiguous. On the map produced by the West, the wall is no more than a shaded line, lost in the proliferation of prosaic, more politically neutral information. On the East

German map, the territory of the West is entirely unmarked, a white expanse as unknown and as exterior as the open sea on charts made long ago when the world was still known to be flat. These two maps tell their stories separately; each expresses its own distinct political illusion. Measured as geometry, the interior appears to be West Berlin. But the enforced interior is the East—an isolated urban prison that paradoxically surrounded the "free" space. Outside was *contained* by inside.

Peter Schneider's novel *The Wall Jumper*, published in 1983, features the Wall itself as its literary protagonist. The author's tone is wryly nonpartisan, and the cast of characters, neatly caricatured, are mere instruments and evidence of Berlin's complex identity. Throughout the novel, interior and exterior exchange roles. The narrator tells the story of Mr. Kabe, a West Berliner who made fifteen successful jumps *toward* the East, even though he would have been free to pass through the legal checkpoints.

> He ignored the calls of officials trying to explain to him which was East and which was West. The interrogators could think of no better explanation for this extraordinary reversal in direction than that Kabe had several screws loose. They sent him to the psychiatric clinic at Buch, but the doctors could find nothing wrong with him, other than a pathological desire to overcome the Wall. Kabe enjoyed a special position at the clinic as a blockade runner whose jump had defined the points of the compass anew.[33]

These are lines of escape that resist not simply the political limits themselves, but the mythology of those limits. Kabe turns the geometry of legislated space inside out, much in the way that Walter Benjamin, decades earlier in the same city, exposed the myth of interiority as child's play.

Among the nightshirts, aprons and undershirts which
were kept there in the back was the thing that turned the
wardrobe into an adventure for me. I had to clear a way
for myself to its farthest corner. There I would come upon
my socks, which lay piled in traditional fashion—that is
to say, rolled up and turned inside out. Every pair had
the appearance of a little pocket. For me, nothing surpassed
the pleasure of thrusting my hand as deeply as possible
into its interior. I did not do this for the sake of the pocket's
warmth . . . but when I had brought out "the present,"
"the pocket" in which it had lain was no longer there.
I could not repeat the experiment on this phenomenon
often enough. It taught me that form and content, veil
and what is veiled, are the same.
—Walter Benjamin, *A Berlin Childhood*

To Benjamin as a child, the disappearance of his socks' interior
seemed a conjurer's trick. Like the perverse topology of Felix Klein's
bottle,[34] the elusive pocket defied any apparent logic of interior/exte-
rior relationships. There was a game to be played again and again,
and never in quite the same way twice. The simple instructions liber-
ated the manner of play, and for this reason the quest inside his wardrobe provided young Benjamin with endless entertainment. His
active desire to possess the interior repeatedly erased the very space
that was the subject of his search. This seemingly naive parable suggests
the paradox of an interior set free by its excessively soft geometry.

Decades later, in an essay on the Italian city of Naples coau-
thored with Asja Lacis, Benjamin again pursued that phenomenon of
an inside seeking to become (then becoming) its exterior. He
described elements of Neapolitan building and topography as indis-
cernible from one another: cellars and natural grottos at the base of
deep crevices, staircases and cliffs rising up from where the city met
the sea. Benjamin contrasts the form of "house" in its Nordic sense

(a structure with explicit, inviolable domestic interiority) with the rambling tenement blocks of Naples, where the dramas of daily life exited the domestic interior onto a public stage. He emphasizes that dramatic action is critical to this interpenetration of private and public zones: "Porosity results not only from the indolence of the Southern artisans, but also, above all, from the passion for improvisation, which demands that space and opportunity be at any price preserved."[35] Much like the maddeningly ambiguous footwear of his childhood, the streets of Naples refuse to be codified by a formal separation of interior from exterior. The idea of public space in the tradition of the large piazza (San Marco in Venice, for example) is replaced by an informal honeycomb of fine-grained interstices—staircases, doorways, balconies, halls, porches, and narrow streets—in which layers of urban and domestic territories blur not only the physical condition of the craggy city but its social stratification as well.[36] It is no coincidence that Benjamin discovered in Naples a congruence between the city's physical tapestry and its society, wherein elements of minor lawlessness were interwoven into the more innocent patterns of quotidian life.

"Harry," she said, "You're outdoors! How funny of you."
And it is true, Park Villas with its vaunted quarter-acre lots
and the compulsory barbeque chimneys does not tempt its
residents outdoors, even the children in summer: In the
snug brick neighborhood of Rabbit's childhood you were
always outdoors, hiding in hollowed-out bushes, scuffling
in the gravel alleys, secure in the closeness of windows
from at least one of which an adult was always watching.
Here, there is a prairie sadness, a barren sky raked by
slender aerials. A sky poisoned by radio waves. A desolate
smell from underground.
—John Updike, *Rabbit Redux*

Outdoors, out of doors, out the door. *Door* shares its Indo-European root **dhwer* with *forest*. This linguistic kinship suggests that the two words functioned similarly in early language—that they referred to the nondomestic, the (door)way out, toward the (forest) hunting ground.[37] In spite of their textural complexity, forests resist segmentation. A forest is a smoothish space dense with details and ecological interdependencies; in the atlas of symbolic environments, it is a primary domain of the lost and the unknown. It is uncultivated, uncivilized, outside the house, and outside the agrarian landscape. Even more, the forest is outside the city. Its very "otherness" leads toward a fresh if unstable image of exteriority. In the realm of minor architectures, all doors lead outward toward the forest, away from the inexorable domestication through which all sense of the original, primordial forest has been erased.

To be "out of doors" is (ostensibly) to breach the segmented interior; yet in Updike's second *Rabbit* novel Harry Angstrom's physical location cannot transcend his essentially interiorized condition. He is caught in a hard segment, an unfluid space insidiously constructed through a set of cultural paradigms that emerged in the United States in the decades following the Second World War. Harry's memory of a childhood replete with outdoor hiding places, alleys, and surrogate family keeping him safe invokes a granular texture reminiscent of Benjamin's Naples. But his grownup house manifests an interior in which he is captured and metaphorically incarcerated through paradigms of "success," "upward mobility," and "progress." Each of these establishes its own segmentations, its set of unbreachable interiors.

It is perhaps ironic that the development of this segmentation and erasure of the outside was perpetrated through legislation with an opposite agenda—the smoothing of our continental nation-space through the Interstate Highway Act of 1956.[38] This massive construction effort, as grand a public works project as any of the New Deal, was concurrent with the escalation of the Cold War, a war that capitalized on anticipation of an atomic event to gain public approval for the expenditure. The federal government commissioned a web of asphalt corridors from coast to coast and border to border, part Baron

Haussmann, part Robert Moses on a grander scale. Connecting all major cities to one another, these interstate highways were calibrated to accommodate a great exodus from metropolitan targets and to facilitate the movement of troops and materials across the country—should the Cold War specter of nuclear holocaust occur. The highways in turn engendered the development of farmland into hard segments of shopping malls with their attendant oceans of parking, and new suburban municipalities with their tentacled dead ends. Like the interstate roads, suburban streets were planned wider than the intimate neighborhoods warranted, again for the purpose of hasty evacuation. Yet these streets and yards are not fluid, nor do they tempt their residents outdoors.

Harry's neighborhood of Penn Villas is in Pennsylvania, the state named for the woods of William Penn. Penn's sylvan landscape is conspicuously absent, the original forest having given way first to agricultural production, then in the postwar years to an explosion of developments like those of William Levitt. The several Levittowns and their immediate progeny were euphorically lauded and embraced for their affordability (the G.I. Bill), community (good schools), and safe, friendly, accessible outdoors. But by 1970 Updike's canny eye perceived that "prairie sadness" in an outdoors empty not only of woods but of *any* kind of life. Why indeed had Harry ventured outside? He may have been momentarily lured there by subliminal memories of a primordial forest that no longer existed.[39] Perhaps he intuitively rebelled against an interiority firmly insulated from the exterior world, for his larger predicament includes a lack of empathy with his own domestic rooms, in which a "slippery disposable gloss"[40] repels any human encounter. The American suburb, particularly as it developed in the 1970s and '80s,[41] may be the consummate striated space.

> Whenever humanity seems condemned to heaviness, I
> think I should fly like Perseus into a different space.
> —Italo Calvino, *Six Memos for the Next Millennium*

Interiors are heavy, weighted by gravity on all sides. Flight is an exit from gravity, a defiance of enclosure. A popular image these days, accessible through a digital search engine, is that of literal "lines of flight" strung across the global map, lines that connect airport to airport, city to city.[42] These lines are manifest in real time. They constitute a diagram that challenges every geographical interior—physically constructed, politically legislated, and geologically evolved. Lines of flight are transgressions of interiority; their multiplicity generates a uniquely fluid space that, though vast, is minoritarian. Invisible to any system that defines space in terms of fixed geometry, measurability, and materiality, these lines cannot be reduced to laws of space or laws of time. They are lines of pure escape.

If we acknowledge the mythic figure of Daedalus as the original architect of Western tradition,[43] then the first architecture of escape (also a literal line of flight) is the escape of the first architect. Daedalus is the architect of at least four major works: hollow cow, labyrinth, dancing floor, and feathered wings. The first is an interior disguised within an animal/object made of wood, in which the cursed queen Pasiphae could conceal her shameful lust. Hidden within the hollow cow, she safely approached and coupled with the bull that was the object of her desire. Their illicit child was the Minotaur who became, in turn, the object of Daedalus's second work of architecture when King Minos enjoined his architect to construct a labyrinth from which the beast could not escape.[44] These first two works were interiors with explicit centers, commissioned by Minos to bury and conceal his own deviances (his offense to Poseidon, his consequently cursed wife, his monstrous stepson). He authorized these interiors to maintain his sprawling sovereignty. In contrast, Daedalus's third construction—a dancing floor (*choros*) for Ariadne—is an architecture without an interior, a pattern wrought (or woven) to encourage the continual cycle of making and remaking space. For the *choros* is not only a floor for dancing; it is also the dance itself.[45]

When Ariadne gave to Theseus a thread that allowed him to penetrate the labyrinth, kill the Minotaur, and then escape, the king blamed Daedalus and incarcerated him and his son Icarus within that very same labyrinth. The architect thus became prisoner in the prison of his own design. From within the labyrinth, Daedalus conceived his fourth great work. Neither object nor interior, it was a machine that defied the very concept of interior, an apparatus designed explicitly for escape.[46] Centuries before Leonardo da Vinci made his speculative drawings of flying machines, mythical Daedalus fabricated wings of feathers and wax; he and his son flew up and out of the enclosure, which had no roof. With hindsight we can claim that they violated the rules of perspective that assume a level, solid, and steady ground separated from the amorphous sky by a horizon, and a point on the horizon to which all lines of sight converge. For Icarus, the escape was only a foreshadowing of his fall to death, thus condemning his father to yet another (metaphorical) prison of mourning and isolation.

The nineteenth century can lay claim to an emerging philosophy of the interior,[47] the twentieth century to a multidisciplinary assault on all that interiority represented. Following the publication of Freud's *The Interpretation of Dreams* in 1899, the development of psychiatry as a formal discipline challenged the privacy of mind with a medical rationale for bringing all one's interior thoughts (even the hidden matter of dreams) out into the light and space of day.[48] In the 1950s the French novelist Alain Robbe-Grillet advocated a similar transformation for literature, writing a manifesto that called for replacing the richness of plot and character that had defined the novel in the nineteenth century with flattened narratives of pure sur-face.[49] In Robbe-Grillet's own novels, the distinct strata formerly thought necessary to produce literary antagonisms give way to a sin-gle plane, a continuous and transparent canvas that preempts both private obsessions and dispersed interiors.

Architecture too professed to join this emerging trend toward transparency, which became one of modernism's expressions of vir-tue. But despite their rhetorical claims, modern architects failed to construct a fundamental challenge to interiority. Instead, their uto-pian visions postulated another kind of interior, a closed set of formal principles that were idealized, self-referential, and static. Symmetries and centers, with their attendant hierarchies, continued to prevail, and these preserved their interiors absolutely. Power relies on such centered and concentric diagrams.[50] Through the latter half of the twentieth century and into the twenty-first, buildings have contin-ued to hold their interiors hostage, even when given skins of glass. Once within the orbit of these structures, it is impossible to gain the outside. A state of interiority has been written into the codes of both their spaces and their politics.

Architecture in a minor mode will necessarily render its interi-ors contingent, diminished, and fragile. In this state, interior space can no longer oppose exterior; it emerges onto the threshold of *becoming* exterior. Thus exteriority is a state that remains elusive, that can never be fully realized. A perceived exterior becomes the next interior; we are always in pursuit of an exit, desiring an outside. The spatial version of such desiring has hardly been tested.

Perhaps the architect Piranesi had a similar vision in the eigh-teenth century, when he made his *Carceri d'invenzione* etchings.[51] In most of the series there are no prisoners except the viewer, whose gaze seeks a route of escape from the distorted perspective, multiple van-ishing points, and lack of a horizon. These spaces are contiguous and

held together by their Kafkan contradictions, including an absence of exits. The drawings are prophetic not of future architectural spaces per se, but of a post-Cartesian state of mind. Though written in lines rather than words, they nevertheless construct a narrative about the emerging potential for architectural relativity. And while the compositions are perceived as more interior than exterior (the reference to prison certainly suggests their territory as bounded), these interiors have no limits. Space flies off in every direction, but without clear lines of flight. Vanishing points contradict the rules of classical geometry and lie far off the margins of the page. Outside is not straight ahead; it is around corners, up stairs, across bridges—invisible, elusive, and likely unattainable.

Piranesi's vertiginous interiors challenge the myth of interiority; they even seem to anticipate the beginning of the end of the interior. It is impossible to imagine an architectural object that can contain them.

THE MYTH OF THE OBJECT

> Ownership is the most intimate relationship that one can
> have to objects. Not that they come alive in him; it is he
> who lives in them.
> —Walter Benjamin, "Unpacking My Library"

> All visible objects, man, are but as pasteboard masks.
> —Herman Melville, *Moby Dick*

On that ubiquitous sea of our reluctant present float the visible objects
of architecture. They drift along highways and across hillsides; they
anchor whole city blocks.[1] In magazines they can incite an alternative
sexual energy; in catalogs they exhibit the newest, thinnest, and shin-
iest commodities of the construction industry. At metropolitan
fringes they are barges of stuff in oceans of parking; in urban centers,
attenuated to pierce the clouds. In spite of their often-stated transparency, their interiors hide behind mirrored facades. What lies con-
cealed beneath these material masks, and how might we shake the
hidden matter free?

While the assault on the interior is through mechanisms of
escape as lines of flight, an object can be exhausted *by* its interior. The
myth of the architectural object is inevitably tied to its own fundamental, nonspatial capture—its closed identity as a commodity and

its function as currency. It is made solid by these attributes. To subvert the object myth is necessarily to subtract both the commodity identity and the currency function from an object, to deobjectify through physical, political, and syntactical means. Vibrations, set in motion by latent desires that reside deep within pyramids of corporate or totalitarian power, may weaken an object's solidity and fracture its singularity. These politicized forces, more even than escapes from the spatial interior, tend to take place *in* place; architectural objects respond to lines of force, but not necessarily through lines of flight. They atomize; *forms* transform to *fields.*[2]

Interior may be to exterior as red is to green, but object is to field as red is to not red; the two cannot coexist within the same space. Every object becomes the definitive center of the space around it, but the essence of a field is its absence of center, of symmetry, and of hierarchy.[3] Fields are precursor to the nets and webs that now consume our global spatial imagination. These conceptual forms of space emerged around 1910,[4] when developments in the arts and sciences shattered a certain model of space that had prevailed since the Renaissance. During the decade that followed, the futurist group in Italy dematerialized objects by introducing the energy of motion; they *inserted* the dimension of time and the aura of speed into the space of the object. At around the same time, cubist painters in France reduced the object and the space around it to a nonhierarchical assemblage of flattened fragments;[5] they *eliminated* the idea of center and the dimension of depth. In physics, Einstein's papers of 1905 and 1915 unite these two transformations within a conceptual space-time continuum in which "field" refers both to a region of space and to the laws that control the relations in that region (for example, a gravitational field). Physics, literature, music, and the visual arts (but not architecture) introduced and embraced these highly unstable and relative fields, upsetting both Cartesian laws of space and Newtonian laws of motion.

Words move, music moves
Only in time; but that which is only living
Can only die. Words, after speech, reach
Into the silence. Only by the form, the pattern,
Can words or music reach
The stillness, as a Chinese jar still
Moves perpetually in its stillness.
—T. S. Eliot, *Four Quartets*

Eliot's Chinese jar is not the first vessel-object[6] to figure as a dominant character in a poem. Keats's Grecian urn tells the story of Platonic Beauty wedded to Truth,[7] and Wallace Stevens's jar in Tennessee
"tamed / the slovenly wilderness" and "took dominion everywhere."
But Eliot's jar rejects such philosophical and spatial authority. Making no claim to either truth or power, it "moves perpetually in its stillness." Its vibrations are speech at its most primitive; Deleuze might
have said that the jar began to stutter.[8] Or, in Kafka's universe, it
might emit nearly silent sounds like the incessant humming of the
mouse Josephine. At the threshold of relinquishing all objectivity and
object status, the vessel is actively becoming contingent. Like the
prose of *Finnegans Wake* that hums along for over 600 pages, Eliot's
jar represents twentieth-century cultural transformations in which
motions replace meaning, and sounds replace sense.

Around the same time that Eliot set his Chinese jar a-trembling,
certain social conditions in Europe were already threatened by those
"diabolical powers" at Kafka's door. Within the next three decades,
particular expressions of minoritarian space emerged from within
those demonic structures—in subversive underground tactics of the
Jews of the Warsaw ghetto as German troops patrolled the streets
above, in communications through prison walls in the Soviet gulags.[9]
Eliot's Chinese jar only tenuously retains its object status. No longer
singular, it is consumed by patterns (which is to say, repetitions); it

approaches an indeterminate and nearly fluid state. Eliot has offered us a poetic representation of language's (or architecture's) endless possibilities for producing multiplicity, and for becoming minor.

> The village lay under deep snow. There was no sign of the Castle hill, fog and darkness surrounded it, not even the faintest gleam of light suggested the large Castle. K. stood a long time on the wooden bridge that leads from the main road to the village, gazing upward into the seeming emptiness.
> —Franz Kafka, *The Castle*

We turn again to Kafka, as the land surveyor K. arrives at an unnamed village in late evening. Above looms the Castle/object, invisible but powerful, both architectural structure and parent authority beneath which all other objects reside. Its sovereignty is mythic, unseen. Connected to its mystique is the figure of Klamm who, like Orwell's Big Brother, governs by reputation rather than by manifestations of physical force. The object (Castle) and the objectification of authority (Klamm's image) merge. Throughout the novel (and in spite of its impoverished language) this power dominates. Objects are mute, communication is an illusion, and telephones reduce language to noise. As the Chairman explains to K., "All those contacts are merely apparent. . . . Here on our local telephones we hear that constant telephoning as a murmuring and singing, you must have heard it too. Well this murmuring and singing is the only reliable thing that the local telephones convey to us, everything else is deceptive."[10] Unlike the setting of *The Trial*, which approximates the texture of a European city (Prague perhaps), the village at the base of the Castle is allegorical, generic, and remote—a place of exile.[11] It is less a segmented space than a single hard segment, a pyramidal object of law with Klamm and the Castle at the top.

Much of the novel takes place at the Gentleman's Inn, where K. finds lodging on his first night in the village. Unlike the sealed, claustrophobic chambers of *The Trial*, rooms at the Inn are drafty; noise and air penetrate everywhere. Nevertheless the space feels full, dense with the weight of paper documents. These form a heavy, singularly impenetrable block—a meta-object that complements (but does not mirror) the invisible authority of the Castle itself.[12] While the spaces within *The Trial* engage the architectonics of doorways, courtrooms, banks, staircases, and corridors, *The Castle* comprises an infinite redundancy of files and folders. *The Trial* is a landscape of nested and frozen interiors; *The Castle* is the objectification of that space, constructed of the literal *materials* of bureaucracy, not its processes. At the Inn, guest rooms along the corridor are only tenuously defined. There is no privacy. Doors, like those of toilet stalls, stop short of the floor and ceiling. Within each room men sit in their beds, working endlessly and unproductively through dense stacks of paper. The documents make solid what would otherwise be interior space. A person can scarcely squeeze through; there is no vacancy at this inn.

—————————

By destroying all space between men and pressing men against each other, even the productive potentialities of isolation are annihilated.
—Hannah Arendt, *The Origins of Totalitarianism*

The same kind of authority that particularizes and frames an interior for its own purposes constructs an object not only as a physical form, recognizable by its shape, iconography, and intent, but also as an object-system, a body of law that prescribes all relationships, including spatial ones. This kind of system is a sanctioned construction of ordered experience, the law of life lived. It is here that we might distinguish the Nazi regime and its spatial products as a particular form of totalitarian project. While Stalinist/Soviet space (for example) was defined by its systematic construction of limited, interior, and opaque rooms of propagandized thought (the kinds of spaces and language that Orwell made so explicit in *Nineteen Eighty-four*), the Nazi project established no interior at all; rather, it reconstructed human identities into object-relations.

In the Castle's shadow is the camp.[13] For the German state to establish sovereignty, it had to create the specific social relation of nationalism by objectifying through exclusion all bodies that did not belong to the idealized nation. The concentration and extermination camps emerged through this form of reason. In the camps, inmates' names were replaced with numbers. Instead of producing segmentation, this indexing served to erase all distinction between individuals and to make of the assemblage a singular block—the result of an inflexible process of rationalization. Like the masses of files at the Gentleman's Inn, the numbered bodies in the camps transformed the space of the barracks figuratively into a single object, solidifying (and consequently erasing) both the interior and the humanity within. Objectification, in this sense, is not merely the stripping of humanity and human relations from individuals; it is also the process by which the elemental object (in this case the population of camp inmates) *hides* human relations and qualities. The distinction is important because it allows us to identify this process within the larger circulating economy. An object at the end of a rationalized production line masks the very identities that produced the object. In the camps, the crowd itself *became* (rather than produced) the final object. In this particular process of objectification, "crowd" was assigned a (negative) value achieved only through its destruction. Extermination followed objectification; it was not people but a perceived *other* that was being destroyed—that which was not the *Volk*.

Segregation is one method of spatial control; crowding is another.[14] The first is the method of the prison, or the official segmentation of cities in times of plague.[15] The second is the means employed in concentration camps. When space is crowded with bodies, it becomes itself an object that conceals each individual *subject*, and even conceals the visible object that *is* the human body. As Arendt suggests, communication requires distance. Eliminating space between people precludes communication and all its attendant humanity. It is a process that objectifies *through abstraction*. The Nazi holocaust is a particularly explicit example of this phenomenon, because it was repeatedly made spatial through the crowding into enclaves, into train cars, into barracks, into chambers full of lethal gas.[16]

> On Friday evenings, in that crowded kitchen, the tiny
> table was spread with a cloth and two candles glowed on
> an overturned plate. An air of Sabbath eve festivity
> pervaded that cramped space, reminding me of my
> childhood home.
> —Vladka Meed, *On Both Sides of the Wall*

Within the city of Warsaw, a different mode of crowding preceded the "relocation to the east." The Jewish Residential Quarter[17] was publicly announced on Yom Kippur in 1940; a month later the ghetto was sealed. This small section of the city became home to nearly 400,000 people. It was seemingly a place of no exit, a walled enclave. Over the next year the population was continually reduced through deportations; but as the area was made progressively smaller in four separate stages, the extreme density persisted. Within houses, even within walls, the construction of hiding places developed into a thriving industry.[18] These too were spaces without exit, blocks within blocks, individually conceived, frozen, and isolating. But as German troops continued the process of round-ups and deportations, the group of Jews committed to forceful resistance dug out irregular bunkers below ground. "Seemingly overnight, the ghetto, particularly in the central area, had become a city on two levels—houses above ground, and cellars and tunnels below."[19] Here the subtle architectural reverberations that we call *minor* found opportunities. To preserve an effective network of communication, the members of the underground group excavated tunnels *between* bunkers, and in some instances managed to tunnel through to meet with sympathizers on the Aryan side of the wall.[20] Over a period of several months, the plan of the ghetto's underground complex was in a continual state of evolution, of perpetual constructions and deconstructions. Politicized literally from below, these shifting asymmetries and a constantly evolving system of exits allowed the Jews of Warsaw to survive as long as they did.[21]

Deleuze and Guattari say of minor literature that "its cramped space forces each individual intrigue to connect immediately to politics."[22] In their context, "cramped space" is a metaphor; in the ghetto it was literal. But in each case, the same condition that precludes political action also authorizes a new space in which such action can occur. This paradox unfolds within a matrix of gestures that build toward resistance. A resistance to equilibrium—an urge to be improper and to desecrate—can bind human desire to architectural acts. Architecture that supports violence (the torture chamber) is thus translated into violence *upon* architecture (the violation of the chamber). Hidden beneath the overt politics of the State is the latent, perhaps original, "politics" with which we are concerned: forces that unpack captured time and unfold the hidden spatial relations bound within objects. In the Warsaw ghetto, politics was removed from the nexus between law and violence (law-sustaining or law-creating) and returned to the nexus between humanity and violence—Benjamin's "divine violence."[23]

A state of exception exists as a condition bound to sovereignty.[24] Now let us imagine a *space* of exception that emerges in opposition to the sovereign State.[25] It is a paradox of Agamben's theory of bare life,[26] with its reduction of all that is human to the merest conditions for survival, that these extreme conditions of lack force open the cracks within which resistance can take hold. True resistance is never an intellectual move; it is a physical, spatial response to the intersection of authority and immanence. This is to say that minor architectures open within a seemingly opaque object system an entirely different order of experience, an entirely new *nomos* as a spatial text. Hence a space of exception arises at the threshold of bare life, *from within the very State that prohibits its existence*. The authority of the state of exception to exclude such space is overturned.

> The kitchen on one side, the living room on the other, are visible. The furniture that frames his life looks Martian in the morning light: an armchair covered in synthetic fabric enlivened by a silver thread, a sofa of airfoam slabs, . . . a piece of driftwood that is a lamp, nothing shaped directly for its purpose, gadgets designed to repel repair, nothing straight from a human hand, furniture Rabbit has lived among but never known, made of substances he cannot name, that has aged as in a department store window, worn out without once conforming to his body.
> —John Updike, *Rabbit Redux*

How is it that we can so fluidly move from the Nazi concentration camps in Poland to Harry Angstrom's living room in suburban Pennsylvania? These contexts seem unbridgeable: fascism and capitalism, old world and new, extermination and upward mobility. On one side, cremation ovens surrounded by barbed wire; on the other, detached houses surrounded by manicured lawns. The quintessentially American suburban paradigm (though now globally ubiquitous) seems at an opposite pole from the horrors of Auschwitz.[27] Yet these systems are each fabrications of their respective regimes, and every regime produces objects that further its agenda.[28] Camp and suburb each has its inmates, its victims.

The close of World War II ironically precipitated an American ideology in which the objectification of property redefined the new-world democratic ideal.[29] Property (which included a mortgaged house, suites of matching furniture, two cars, and sometimes a swimming pool) became ever more intently commodified. Houses became "homes" and gardens became "yards";[30] the land surrounding the house also became an object of ownership. Its value was simultaneously heavy and abstract—heavy because it occupied space and abstract because in its new nonagrarian state it had become essentially useless. Thus were the productive spaces of both house and garden stripped of their former material and spatial qualities, and repackaged as products. Within that house that "does not tempt its residents outdoors," Harry Angstrom is imprisoned in alienation and discomfort, surrounded by those mysterious objects of mysterious "substances he cannot name" that he, like everyone, has been coerced to consume. He does not own them in the intimate sense that Walter Benjamin owns his books; *they* own *him*.

These commodities claim space, but what space exactly?[31] It is space absent of use, but is it not also space without time, without occasion?[32] For the producer, objects structure time into a rational matrix of production efficiencies; but for the consumer, objects *freeze* time. Once taken home (or at a larger scale, once the home is acquired), an object's allure is replaced by the deadening weight of its presence, and a dread of its immanent obsolescence.[33] For all objects, ends justify means. Just as every child longs for the end of the journey ("Are we there yet?"), every client longs for the end of construction ("When will it be finished?"). Eventually, though often not soon enough, the ribbon is cut. A photographer is called in. Materials and construction techniques are praised for their lifespan, and products are warranted for twenty years. Necessary maintenance and repairs are considered signs of failure. Thus consumed, the object is closed to question. We are there, finished; time has been explicitly vanquished. This makes an object weigh heavily.

Buildings represent a multiplicity of powers congealed to form a single weighty object with a singular power, whose authority is, above all else, to repel change. Perhaps we could say that the overwhelming weight of an architectural object is this stated ability to resist change, which is, after all, the most predictable constant of our world. Frozen in that illusion of being and remaining complete, buildings produce an ironic and subliminal longing for their own different futures.

"Honored guests! I have, admittedly, broken a world record. If, however, you were to ask me how I have achieved this, I could not answer adequately. Actually, I cannot even swim. I have always wanted to learn, but have never had the opportunity. How then did it come to be that I was sent by my country to the Olympic Games? This is, of course, also the question I ask of myself. I must first explain that I am not now in my fatherland and, in spite of considerable effort, cannot understand a word of what has been spoken."
—Franz Kafka, "Fragment"

The segmented American landscape can be understood as an apparatus composed of objects: automobiles throttling down a divided freeway, reticent houses discrete from neighbors and street, captive waters of private pools.[34] A great spatial paradox of the United States is that its original, rootless, and rhizomatic character so evident in the cultural practices of the Native Americans was aggressively segmented by the descendants of European settlers. "America" is a land developed to fulfill dreams; but these dreams have tended increasingly toward illusions, becoming indistinguishable from the object/commodities that so effectively replaced the originally intended, intangible and fluid new-world values of liberty and happiness.

And where are these illusory dreams made more vulnerable than at an inward-facing backyard cocktail party, surrounded by one's upwardly mobile neighbors and friends? It is here that we meet Neddy Merrill in John Cheever's story "The Swimmer." No foreshadowing of melancholy mars Neddy's inspiration to swim home across Westchester County. On a perfect summer day at the euphoric end of an afternoon, he imagines the rectangles of backyard pools merged into a fluid stream leading home: "He seemed to see, with a cartographer's eye, that string of swimming pools, that quasi-subterranean stream that curved across the county. He had made a discovery, a contribution to modern geography; he would name the stream Lucinda after his wife."[35]

And so Neddy sets out on his journey along the Lucinda River. Over the next hours, he passes through successive states: striated spaces and smooth ones. The first state is the condition of the Westchester County neighborhood itself, segmented in spite of its convivial, neighborly pretensions. (Backyard gatherings provide an illusion of community; in reality, they manifest the most competitive aspects of that culture: the beauty and thinness of the wives, the quality and names of the drinks, the flaunting of planned vacations, the arrogance of infidelities.) The second state of architecture emerges in Neddy's imagination as a smooth, continuous space; with the invention of the stream Lucinda, he attempts to correct the segmented assemblage, to erase the blocks. He approaches this vision with confident abandon. Yet the waters turn progressively colder; a busy road proves a dangerous obstruction. As Neddy makes his way from house to house, pool to pool, friend to former friend, he understands less and less of what he sees and hears. The segmented condition reconvenes. Like Kafka's Great Swimmer, he is a stranger within his own language. Over the course of an afternoon (or perhaps as much as a decade), Neddy's tour through backyards and social circles seems to confirm his habitual behaviors, even as it abets his heightened state of exclusion.

Neddy's swim is denial set against and within a matrix of capture: the risk of revealing oneself, the loss of suburban social graces, the possibility of bankruptcy and foreclosure, and the breakdown of his seemingly ideal family structure. He wants to sublimate the private pools into a flowing river, to have these private enclosures take into full account what has happened to him, to remove from these objects their boundaries. Swimming through—that is to say, entering into—a series of private properties, Neddy attempts to draw a fluid line of force, but finds himself blocked by a sequence of ossified, fortified interiors. To enter them, he must assume certain behaviors: the flirtatious, confident, leisurely swagger of the County. Thus the sense of well-being that provoked him to embark on his swim is endangered by the very context that becomes for him a foreign territory. His construction is an illusion. In fact, over the course of his swim, the blocks become ever more discontinuous, segmented by boundaries of time as well as space. As hours lengthen into years, he is estranged by the very temporalities that should hold his daily life in place. Though space is the agency and theater of action, he is ultimately a victim of duplicitous time.

If a fool's paradise is a wise man's hell, Neddy would appear to have sacrificed everything for wisdom. Like Kafka's fleet-footed messenger, he is trapped within temporal discontinuities. As if in that dream state of running without covering any ground, his forward motion is frustrated by his past transgressions. The machine-like nature of his swim, climbing out of one pool and running toward another, might reach a smooth state were it not for the social, economic, and architectural obstructions that prevent fluidity. His tour is not an escape so much as it is an attempt at reassimilation; but to assimilate requires the destruction of the partitioned objects. Yet he finds that the objects' boundaries are inviolable; no amount of bare-chested youthful charm can draw a seamless line across the territory, for the very power of Westchester County *depends* on its segmentation. And so in spite of Neddy's riparian vision, the boundaries of the yards cannot be breached. Lot lines act with vengeful exaggeration, manning the barricades. By the time he reaches what he thinks is home, years have passed; his neighbors have scorned and shamed him for his weakness and indiscretions; his house is in ruined abandon and his wife and daughters have disappeared. This is the final archi-tecture of the story: the return to blocks in the form of segmented time. Poor Neddy falls victim to a certain kind of commodity power that renders smoothness impossible.

Delight in Blindness.
—Friedrich Nietzsche, *The Gay Science*

If, as Melville says, "objects are but as pasteboard masks," then blind-ness may reveal what the object hides. At the exact center of T. S. Eliot's "The Waste Land" is Tiresias, the blind prophet who can see "the substance of the poem."[36] What is this substance? It is a *tex*ture not readily apparent from the poem's linear structure and its segmen-tation into five discrete, separately titled sections. Tiresias is, as Eliot says, "a mere spectator and not indeed a 'character,' [and] yet the most important personage in the poem, uniting all the rest."[37] He is the fluid force that reveals the poem's minor dimension; the indeter-minate center and its blind occupant are measures of smooth space that reshape the architecture of the poem from within.

To think of blindness and of architecture is also to think of Jorge Luis Borges, the blind Argentine author whose fictions have so engaged our spatial imagination. Kafkan space sets the stage for the Borgesian worlds of libraries and labyrinths, and Borges once directly stated, "Well, I felt that I owed so much to Kafka that I really didn't need to exist."[38] Yet his universe is different from Kafka's; his fiction combines a pure imaginary with a vast storehouse of literary and historical references. The architecture within his stories challenges conventional geometries more (and also less) than Kafka's politicized constructions. Borges invents entire worlds; his characters are subverted not by their inability to act but by the absolute nature of the spatial abstractions that surround them—vaguely urban, quasi-historical, partly literary situations in which Ariadne's mythic thread becomes hopelessly tangled in repetitive, impossible warps of space and time.

Borges's essays and stories are an unfolding of his own preoccupations through the writers and myths that he inherits: not only Kafka but Paul Valéry, Rudyard Kipling, the paradox of Zeno, and the mysteries of Pascal. His fictional "Library of Babel" is a collection of every imaginable text, the ultimate Deleuzian structure whose "center is everywhere and circumference is inaccessible."[39] The architecture of the library is relentlessly repetitive, but the texts themselves are infinitely varied. Each is a minoritarian event within the multiplicity of the library/universe. Nothing is indexed, so content is discovered only by chance, each bit a minor reward within an endless search.

Borges compares the act of reading itself to a wandering journey through the texture of a text; he claims as a nearsighted child to have searched for the minotaur within the maze of letters on a page. Labyrinths—of time as well as space—became a prevailing theme of his stories. His fiction describes only mathematical, generic spatial conditions. We encounter more mirrors than what the mirrors might reveal, more abstractions of stairs and courtyards than concrete evidence of buildings and things. The absence of visual references and the ubiquitous presence of literary texts are directly linked to his affection for words, and his conviction that our visual world is not always congruent with our spatial one.[40] His architecture embodies the space of blindness, relentlessly multidimensional and never pictorial. (By contrast, Kafka's rooms are full of paintings and photographs.) Because for Borges time as well as space is cyclical, we are never sure whether lines of sight go forward or backward. Though there appear to be no lines of flight, there is also a distinct absence of objects. Thus in spite of their singular brand of interiority, architectures in the Borgesian universe bend toward the minor.

Buildings are normally defined by their appearance. For architecture to approach a condition of minority, it must first become not visible. This may happen through the agency of imagination, which, ironically, has no need of the image. The imagination sets the image free; to look with imagination is to forget an object and its meaning, to forget its commodity function, and to become lost in a sightless space where invention, propelled by lines of force, becomes possible.[41] Blindness—as an individual subjective condition—is a partial subtraction from the realm of the sensual, a "forgetting" of the visual. As other senses take over, they blur into one another; they vibrate with intensities and intersect without design, without awareness. This stuttering and meandering of the senses is precisely the condition that reveals human relations. For our purposes, it destroys not only an object's image but also its material limits, its past associations, and its present context—its frozen meaning.

> "Put some people in there now. What's a cathedral
> without people?"
> —Raymond Carver, "Cathedral"

In Carver's story "Cathedral," blindness emerges as a minor agent in the destruction (and reconstruction) of a canonical architectural object; it also *constructs* a relationship between two people, a spatial relation that becomes more powerful than the separate identity of either one. This relation, this new space, destroys the cathedral/object much as the space between Timerman and his fellow prisoner destroys the prison/interior.

When a blind man who is a friend of the narrator's wife is invited to the couple's home for a visit, the host is apprehensive: "I wasn't enthusiastic about his visit. He was no one I knew. . . . Now this same blind man was coming to sleep in my house."[42] He distrusts the blind man; or perhaps he distrusts the condition of blindness itself. For the first part of the evening and through dinner, his wife facilitates the conversation; but eventually she falls asleep on the couch, and the two men are left together in awkward silence. The television is on, a program about the cathedrals of Europe. The host finally asks the blind man, "Do you know what a cathedral looks like? . . . They're really big. . . . They're massive. They're built of stone. Marble, too, sometimes." The blind man asks his new friend to draw a cathedral for him. (Why would he who has no sight ask this?) The host gets a paper bag from the kitchen, and a pencil. He draws a box, a door, a steeple; he describes these object-things with inadequate words, words that refer only to the visible. The cathedral—this particular object far away and its image broadcast through television—is fragmented into a set of known and visual attributes; this necessarily fragments the relation between the two men. And so the object must be withdrawn from its visibility. "'Close your eyes now,' the blind man said to me. I did it. I closed them just like he said."[43] The blind man clasps his own hand around the host's drawing hand as it continues to makes lines on paper. The valence of the entire object and its constituent parts—its flying buttresses, spires, windows, and great hanging doors—is deconstructed through the act of drawing blind. The cathedral is collapsed and yet remarkably reconceived onto the thick brown paper.

Objects simultaneously express human relations and hide them. In "Cathedral" the architectural object is recast and its essence deconstructed—for the blind man's concern is that he cannot see the image. For it to be reimaged onto paper, transformed from its alien strangeness, is to necessarily demonstrate its reality: to transform the object *into a relation*, which is to say, into an object that has de-objectified itself. This erases not only the canonical version of a Gothic cathedral and its singular soaring space, but also the space of a quotidian American living room in which after-dinner drinks and smokes have taken place. No objects remain, nor even any interior. The space engendered through the act of drawing is both deterritorializing and liberating. The narrator concludes, "I was in my house. I knew that. But I didn't feel like I was inside anything. 'It's really something,' I said."[44]

The men's escape into the space of a cathedral is within neither a Euclidean nor even an Einsteinian space; rather, it bleeds into the interstices of Deleuzian strata. This cathedral has separated itself from the historical canon, from all codified scholastic and structural relations. If seen on paper, the drawing will not resemble any known work of architecture; its lines, drawn without the benefit of sight, overlap and intersect in unpredictable ways. The result certainly does not adhere to any conventions of draftsmanship. Yet it satisfies not only the blind man but his sighted host as well. The cathedral as drawn might be compared to Mallarmé's flower—the one "absent from all bouquets" but referring to none in particular.[45] Yet Carver's cathedral cannot remain in the realm of a Mallarméan ideal. The drawing as an image is irrelevant; it is the *act* of drawing that brings the cathedral back—not as an object or even the idea of an object, but as an event.

The penultimate chapter of *The Trial* also takes place in a cathedral. Here the edifice is the figure of the Court—in particular the court of the condemned, for the priest that appears and addresses K. directly by name is the prison chaplain. It is clear at this point that K. has been found guilty. The space of the cathedral has becomes the space of law, and of judgment by law. It is here too that the priest recites to K. the parable "Before the Law" in which, as we have seen, the power of the law-as-object keeps the supplicant frozen for eternity at the gate.

In Carver's story, something opposite takes place. The cathedral acts not as the husk of a building that has appropriated another function, but as an imaginative force that enters into a most prosaic space (living room) and time (after dinner). The cathedral virtually escapes from the towns of France, through the television transmission of the BBC, into the house of an ordinary American and thence to the fingers of a man who cannot see. When the blind man places his hand on the hand of his host, he is asking to be shown "what a cathedral is like," not what it *looks* like. Blind from birth, he has no frame of reference, and may or may not understand the concepts of a spatial interior or a facade. The narrator, with no interest in architecture, has fallen victim to circumstance in two instances, first the arrival of the blind man at his house, and second the coincidence of the television documentary on cathedrals. What does he decide to depict, he who has neither training in architecture nor interest in artistic expression? He does not decide. He closes his eyes, the hand of the blind man riding his own. Denying himself the limits of sight, he deconstructs the cathedral by repositioning his senses. He pulls the pencil across the paper. He *draws*.

The legend of the childishness of my drawing must have originated from those linear compositions of mine in which I tried to combine a concrete image, say that of a man, with the pure representation of the linear element.
—Paul Klee, *On Modern Art*

For architects (and even for painters), drawing is a preamble, a necessary step in practice that leads toward the construction of the "real" work. But Leonardo da Vinci *practiced* in reverse. While still quite young he gave up painting and sculpture and spent the rest of his decades drawing and writing. Lines and words became the means for endless experimentation; his focus went from production to free speculation. Valéry identifies the work in Leonardo's *Notebooks* as the essence of his method, and argues that these drawings are his most potent work. He compares the drawings to a ring of smoke, wherein "a system of altogether interior energies lay claim to a perfect independence and indivisibility. . . . The old is so much utilized, the new so promptly appreciated; and the value of total relationships so clearly re-established, that it seems as though in this realm of pure activity nothing can begin and nothing end."[46] Thus Leonardo is an excellent role model for minor architects. His notebooks full of sketches and notes for unrealized but ambitious ideas are not representations of unbuilt objects; they are both active texts and potent repositories of latent force. In this sense, texts both written and drawn stand *in opposition to* objects. They are nets and fields without beginnings or ends; they de-objectify. Mapped onto a space filled with objects, a text is not a connection among spaces but becomes in itself a singular and complex space that compromises the objects within its scope. (Much of what is written is not textual, because it is has no power.) Through texts, objects can be made to forfeit their symmetry and equilibrium. Texts are lines of force *drawn* with the power to deconstruct.

To *object* (v) to the object (n). To register objections is to draw lines through ~~objects of power~~, objects that are the result of institutions, which in turn rely on knowledge. Knowledge itself is a massive heavy object, with enormous foundations and a reliance on gravity. Theories and philosophies are constructed on the backs of canonical precedents. Like doctrines, they are dangerously authoritarian. Religions, monarchies, systems of law, corporations—these historical patrons of architecture have provided us with the objects upon which minor architects can write (or draw) their objections.

The English word *draw* comes from the root **dhragh*, which it shares with the word *draft*, meaning "to pull." Draft beer is pulled from the tap, the draft horse pulls the wagon, the draftsman pulls the pencil across the page. We draw people out in conversation, we draw conclusions from evidence. A line of force has the same pull as the pull of the draft, the draw, the art of drafting,[47] which is also the *disegno*, the design. The act of drawing a line *through* an object is politicized by the force of the draw. This gives a building new agency.

Decades before Deleuze articulated his theory of the rhizome as a means by which to rethink methods of philosophical inquiry, Paul Klee made rhizomatic drawings. He defined the act of drawing as

"taking a line for a walk."[48] This suggests spontaneity but also continuity. The walking line intersects itself. In Klee's drawings, objects are barely implied, indistinguishable from the fields in which they float without substance or gravity. Pages are unequivocally flat, with no implications of depth. Uniformly textured patterns of lines originate space rather than occupy it. Yet the drawings are precise and deliberate; they have force. Valéry might have said that they are "light like a bird, not like a feather."[49] The drawing that Carver's blind man makes of a cathedral may be much like a drawing by Klee. As draftsmen, the blind man and his host pull the pencil across the page. These lines would likely be notable for their absence of beginnings and ends; they are lines that pass *through* without going *to*.

Minor architectures' lines of force, pulled through existing structures, function much like Deleuze and Guattari's conceptualization of the singing voices in Kafka, voices that deterritorialize language by replacing the solidity of words with vibrato sounds pulled through the vocal chords. Thus attenuated beyond their institutional meanings, these lines (or sounds) express a pure desire.[50] The limit of the language of architecture is this threshold of dematerialization. A minor architecture is *becoming space* rather than *being form*. It hums along restlessly, turning away from the stale auras of commodity, originality, permanence, and perfection, and toward incompleteness and immanance. Klee's reference to the act of drawing as naive, or childish, is in itself illuminating, suggesting that minor architectures might be drawn (pulled, extracted) through a spirit of play.

> One day humanity will play with law just as children play
> with disused objects, not in order to restore them to their
> canonical use but to free them from it for good.
> —Giorgio Agamben, *State of Exception*

Toys and games are two sets of assemblages that claim to facilitate play; but as facilitators they are not equal. Toys are fundamentally nouns—frozen objects severed from the flow of play. A toy's central attribute is its commodity status and its ability to function as an apparatus. The form of a toy determines not just a manner of play but its *limits* of play. A toy is a mere image of play, held in place by empirical features, properties, and trademarks. Unlike Agamben's "disused objects," when a toy enters a disused state (usually soon after its luster fades) there is little hope of liberating it from its intended use. It becomes a waste object.

Games on the other hand are assemblages defined by their *field* of play; without this field they do not exist. A game is fundamentally a verb. Many games need no objects at all. For those that do—the deck of cards, balls of various sizes, discs, tokens, a pair of dice— these things have no *object*ive identity. They are tools, instruments of action to be deployed upon a field. The field is the genesis of the game. Whether chessboard or soccer pitch, it awaits the events that establish its manner of play, which never repeat exactly.[51] Games cannot be objectified.[52] Unlike toys, which as objects mold the individual subject to their nature, games release the individual subject into a collective imaginary. Benjamin's "destructive character" becomes a revolutionary (minor) architect when the act of clearing away is acted within and upon the objects of architecture—not in a wholesale manner of destruction but in a playful manner of de(con)struction.

To play with the laws of architecture and with the disused objects of architecture is to imagine (the major objects of) architecture as a field of play.

THE MYTH OF THE SUBJECT

And the whole earth was of one language, and of one speech.
—Genesis 11:1–9 (King James Version)

Is Ahab, Ahab?
—Herman Melville, *Moby Dick*

The Babel tower was never completed, because collective enunciation died. God saw his subjects' intentions to reach his height; in retribution for their vanity, he dissolved the universal language and caused in its stead a proliferation of unintelligible tongues. Workers were prevented from communicating with one another, and thus unable to coordinate their tasks. "Let us make us a name,"[1] they said; but a name was never found. For poets, painters, and mythologists, the tower in its unfinished state has since become a potent symbol of social disintegration.

For us, the myth of Babel has developed in reverse. Free markets and global competition have made new brands of signature towers that find no difficulty in achieving completion; yet the languages they speak cannot be deciphered. They disguise themselves in costume; they mirror the languages of capital. In the very part of the world where Babel is understood to have been, but on the other side of the Arabian peninsula, the Burj Khalifa tower of Dubai rises to once unattainable heights.[2] In all corners of the world, proliferating architectures speak the specious dialects of their patrons and their authors—a corporate babble far less divine than any biblical edifice might ever have been. Where major buildings once claimed to express the ideals of democracy, they now openly deny a collective value. Their images, like their tenancies, speak to ruthless competition. Rise to power of the *individual* voice has become architecture's strange agenda—authors of the most public art propelled by Godly aspirations. Such efforts rely on superlatives: the ever newer, taller, thinner, brighter, sleeker, more alluringly stunning and photogenic image. Signature buildings not only mirror their corporate (false) prophets, they also become the mechanism for constructing their authors' identities. We can invoke the disembodied voice of the architect Eupalinos in Valéry's Socratic meditation on architecture, saying: "By dint of constructing, I truly believe that I have constructed myself."[3]

There are no subjects except by and for their subjection.
—Louis Althusser, "Lenin and Philosophy"

In contrast to the spatial clarity of the interior and the visible clarity of the object, *subject* is a relentlessly ambiguous concept, fraught with an uncanny ability to pivot toward its opposite. All the way back to its Indo-European root *upo*, the prefix *sub-* has had the duplicitous meanings of "under," "up from under," or "over." Thus it is that subjects occupy positions at both the tops and the bottoms of power structures. But as in any power situation, and particularly those animated by exchanges of capital, what appears to be the subject at the top can be an illusion. Further, in the making of architecture, the roles of architect and client both double again, with the result that it is often unclear *who* is subject to *whom*. The prefix in all its ambiguity privileges relationships over individuals. The idea of subjectivity, with its implications of myriad contingencies, ironically overtakes its own authority and becomes the central figure in dismantling the subject myth.[4]

In fact the elevation of the architect to celebrity status is a relatively recent phenomenon. Formerly, fame came only with the long passage of time; though architects were supported by patrons and some were even publicly acknowledged, their work stood firm beyond them. In a lineage tracing back to Brunelleschi, the last architect in this Renaissance tradition is probably Louis I. Kahn.[5] His iconic stature sprang from a body of work that reflected in built form the presumed virtues of democracy. Kahn's buildings are monumental in the classical sense, marking perhaps the final moment in architecture's history when collective enunciation achieved significance and clarity in physical form. His buildings were not *his*; they belonged to their institutions.[6] In our time "signature" architects have themselves *become* institutions—cultural products commercially distributed much like film icons, or politicians. Contemporary culture has chosen to celebrate individuals and to market their image. Architects wear their buildings the way film stars wear their gowns and politicians their rhetoric. Like politicians, star architects have agendas that are often fundamentally apolitical—founded on the abstract currency of image and the aura of innovation.

Consider the architect-developer in J. G. Ballard's allegorical novel *High Rise*, literally elevated to the top of his own construction. He claims for his major project a vast empty site in London's Docklands, then (in the 1970s) an untapped territory separated from the contingencies of urban life: "For all the proximity of the city two miles away to the west along the river, the office buildings of central London belonged to a different world, in time and space."[7] He finances and designs five identical forty-story towers; the first one completed is the site of the novel. The tower literally embodies a social hierarchy. Lower floors are separated from middle ones by a public level, including a supermarket and swimming pool; the top floors are serviced by their own executive elevators. Stewardesses, teachers, and secretaries live near the ground; above them are the minor executives and doctors. The architect, whose name is Royal, dwells in rarefied and isolated luxury in the penthouse at the top.

The novel opens with this line: "As he sat on his balcony eating the dog, Dr Robert Laing reflected on the unusual events that had taken place within this huge apartment building during the previous three months."[8] This is the endgame in a narrative of social disintegration that parallels the physical disintegration of the building itself. Architect and architecture both support and subvert each other, reflecting a coded hierarchy of class divisions that eventually (in its stubborn resistance to any fluidity) causes both the building and its author to self-destruct. (The sacrificial dog being consumed by Laing in that opening scene is Royal's Alsatian.) Utilities break down, elevators become garbage dumps, and stairwells are taken over as sites of mortal combat. The residents wall themselves in from each other, using furniture as barricades. The *Royal* architect has, in all monarchical willfulness, designed a building that set the strong up against the weak; at one point he leads a hunting party through the interior wilderness. Royal makes his last stand against another tenant (significantly named Wilder) on the penthouse roof. A highly stratified and seemingly ossified architecture has engendered a complete de-evolution, a spatial drama in which primitive survival tactics are acted out on a vertical battlefield.

The *practice* of architecture also has multiple strata, hierarchies of "labor" and "work."[9] In the field: from the carpenter apprentice through the construction foreman to the contractor; in the office: from interns to draftsmen, project architects, and project managers and, at the top, the architect-creator. As architects, we busy ourselves with this narrative of creation. Further, we believe that through our architecture we determine the performances of the "users" who occupy the created spaces.[10] Our ethos is thus framed: the architect-subject establishes (creates) the architecture-object, which in turn determines the manner in which the client uses (behaves in) the space. But this is exactly backward; instead, it is the object that tends toward creating the subject. The subject is only meaningful in relation to the object—they manifest each other in dialectical fashion.[11] Specifically for architects, the building-object constitutes us. We are conditioned to face backward; we squint at the canonized constructions (buildings, styles) that appear to lend structure to our hidden human relations. Whether in overt complicity or aesthetic rebellion, our looking backward is the same. This is to say, we construct ourselves on the dead objects and the dead time of canonized history, which is itself a majority construction. The architect in this way becomes an atomized celebrity, a particle of history's narcissistic mirror. Each building, even if it appears to celebrate the reflection of its author, ironically perpetuates the myths of the majority. What aspires to be different becomes necessarily the same.

The seemingly stable spaces and stable objects that an architect builds are fugitive; they are mere fictive pauses, frozen moments. Space is always under construction, in perpetual loops of distributions and contestations within a latticework of human relations and activity. And it's precisely this complex, cohered fabric within which we must embed ourselves, and thus break the stratified pyramid that holds the architect/subject as a stable identity at the top and the user/subject captive at the bottom. The true subjects of *minor* architectures are these definers and distributors: relations of production, of space and of politics. But since these are relations, they can barely be brought within the category *subject*. In these relational strategies, it is the paradox of the end of the subject that these (minor) architectural acts are the acts of revolutionaries.

Thus to practice architecture in a minor mode requires not only the partial deconstruction of buildings and the structures of power that lead to their incessant reproduction, but also the deconstruction of the architect/subject. Minor architectures not only register a minor voice upon the major one; they also cause *identities* to collapse into one another. Works assumed to be finished are cast back into a state of becoming. Authorship is put into reverse, and the design process becomes editorial, reflecting a composite of blurred identities, a palimpsest of disappearances. It is in this manner that individuals, like interiors, may become deterritorialized. Minor architects leave only their vague reflections behind; the paradox of their architecture is that it leads toward anonymity.

The continual reproduction of space necessarily alternates with its partial deconstruction, which in turn implies a cyclical reproduction and deconstruction of the self. This may seem to weaken the role of the architect; but the dialectical relation between power and weakness is also a culturally constructed narrative. And because the overarching canon for all of these structures of power is rooted in the philosophy of knowledge (which since Foucault has been reframed as a relative system of multiplicities),[12] we return inevitably to Deleuze's assault on that most fundamental canon of all: his repositioning of philosophical inquiry as a fluid, nonlinear, and nonhierarchical process is a guidebook (albeit imprecise) for minor architects.

> To make more pure the language of the tribe.
> —Stéphane Mallarmé, "Tombeau pour Edgar Poe"

Deleuze and Guattari begin *A Thousand Plateaus* with this statement: "The two of us wrote *Anti-Oedipus* together. Since each of us was several, there was already quite a crowd."[13] Thus they neatly write themselves out of the authorial superiority that characterizes the very philosophical tradition that they argue against. Similarly, in his seminal essay "Death of the Author" Roland Barthes constructs an argument for the act of writing as an initiation of the author's disappearance. Here Barthes might well have been speaking of (minor) architecture: "Writing is the destruction of every voice, of every point of origin. Writing is that neutral, composite, oblique space where our subject slips away, the negative where all identity is lost, starting with the very identity of the body of writing." Like Deleuze, Barthes builds an implicit bridge between literature and architecture by acknowledging the particularly spatial nature of a text: "We know now that a text is not a line of words releasing a single 'theological' meaning (the 'message' of the Author-God) but a multi-dimensional space in which a variety of writings, none of them original, blend and clash."[14] This bold claim to an absence of originality positions all writing as a web of quotations, even when they cannot be attributed to individual sources. Barthes alludes to a *babble* of quotations, whose originality lies only in the orchestration of their synthesis and the celebration of their contradictions. We return to the impoverishment of language— the language of repetitions, monosyllables, and stuttering, of words in the process of disintegration. In architecture as in literature, this is language purified of style, language stripped bare.

A collective voice does not arise from the politics of consensus, which after all is only an illusory fabrication of the powerful to incite agreement. Consensus relies on recitation (another form of obedience), a mechanism of power structures that operate from above. A paradox of collective enunciation is that the subversion of the individual poet, or architect, implicitly creates anonymity since it reduces rather than increases visibility. Pablo Neruda captures this phenomenon when he writes, "Tyranny cuts off the singer's head / but the voice from the bottom of the well / returns to the secret streams of the earth / and rises out of nowhere through the mouths of the people."[15] Who expects these voices to express canonical ideas or grammars? Instead, they are undoubtedly primitive in structure, albeit powerful in force. As a challenge to tyranny, Neruda brings voices up *from the bottom*. His deep well is ancestral space, through which tribal voices become pure.

Mallarmé attributes the pure voice of the tribe to the poetry of Edgar Allan Poe;[16] but his sonnet to Poe is also his own *ars poetica*. Mallarmé wanted to substitute an absence of being for being, to replace something with nothing, someone with no one, to dissolve himself and his poems into *le Néant*, the void. For him, it was poetry that had the highest potential to become that empty space of absolute purity. His search for emptiness increased in intensity throughout the development of his oeuvre and became most explicitly spatial in his prose poem *Igitur*.

Igitur is an allegory of collective enunciation acted out in a sequence of archetypal spaces—a vertical "house" that is essentially Leibniz's two-story house in reverse.[17] The poem opens in a tower room, intimate and domestic. Here the title character (who is the last of his tribe) reads from an enormous book the story of his life. As midnight tolls, Igitur closes the volume, blows out the candle,[18] and leaves the chamber. In the second part of the poem, he descends a spiral stair, generating a space of transition as he approaches a subterranean room. His journey down the staircase is one of several thresholds as he approaches a state of multiplicity. At the bottom of the stair (another threshold), he throws a pair of dice as a symbolic act of chance, abdicating both the agency of choice and his own singular identity.[19] He enters a boundlessly vast tomb. Freed of his subjective self, released into a space of immanence, Igitur lies down on the bones of his ancestors.

I live not in myself, but I become
Portion of that around me . . .
—Lord Byron, *Childe Harold's Pilgrimage*, Canto 3

High Rise is not the only novel of J. G. Ballard to feature an architect. But in *Concrete Island* the architect does not rise to the top of his own structure. Like Igitur he descends, and as with Igitur his descent is allegorical. We witness the deconstruction and reconstruction of an architect's identity (not unlike the deconstruction and reconstruction of the cathedral in Carver's story). The central character Maitland is transformed from a man at the top of his profession to a survivor among other survivors—that is, from a major to a minor state. The island space around him abets his metamorphosis.

In the opening scene Maitland is confidently driving one-handed on the M1 motorway, heading west from London, flowing with the traffic away from his mistress and toward his wife, a west-ward line of flight from one woman to another, from London work-place to suburban home. This habitual vector deflects when the swerve of a reckless driver sends his car crashing through a barricade and down a steep embankment. "Shielding his eyes from the sunlight, Maitland saw that he had crashed into a small traffic island, some two hundred yards long and triangular in shape, that lay in the waste ground between three converging motorway routes."[20] Marooned like Crusoe, he is surrounded not by water but by pavement, attended not by a mute Friday but by an equally strange pair of fellow castaways: a tramp named Proctor and a prostitute named Jane.

Days later, after several failed attempts to climb the embankment, Maitland enlists Proctor to help him build a shelter. Though Ballard alludes to his professional life as framed through meetings, budgets, and schedules (an architect mired in the abstractions of architecture rather than its viscera), here Maitland is back to funda-mentals—the design of a primitive hut from the "natural" detritus of civilization. The shelter is an expedient assemblage of rusted car parts, with two engine hoods forming the roof. Over the next days he settles in, assimilates. This assimilation includes both his physical self and his former cultural identities. When he ventures out, "his movement across this forgotten terrain was a journey not merely through the island's past, but through his own." Maitland's desire to escape is waning, as he begins to merge with the landscape around him.

"Architect" and "philanderer" are parts of his former profile; but the accident and his subsequent encounters jostle Maitland from these objectified, cultural identities. Instead of individual agency as a man possessing two women, as a designer of buildings—in short as a man who falsely believes that he determines his surroundings—his material surroundings now determine him. He proceeds to traverse the island, willfully superimposing parts of his body into elements of the landscape that had injured him, in a sense leaving his body behind in pieces:

> Identifying the island with himself, he gazed at the cars in the breaker's yard, at the wire mesh fence, and the concrete caisson behind him. These places of pain and ordeal were now confused with pieces of his body. He gestured toward them, trying to make a circuit of the island so that he could leave these sections of himself where they belonged. He would leave his right leg at the point of the crash, his bruised hands impaled upon the steel fence. He would place his chest where he had sat against the concrete wall. At each point a small ritual would signify the transfer of obligation from himself to the island. He spoke aloud, a priest officiating at the eucharist of his own body. "I am the island." The air shed its light.[21]

Ballard's metaphor here is telling: as day turns to night, Maitland sheds his former coordinates for a new constellation of spatial references set within the boundaries of the island. It is no longer that the physical space presents limits to his escape; within this new framework, escape itself has become meaningless. An escape to what? Back to what? For in Maitland's mind his "home" is the strangest place of all, designed and furnished specifically to repel the comforts of the familiar.[22]

As the novel develops, the space of the island appears to become progressively larger, embracing a geography that includes street patterns, a cemetery, bomb shelters, a movie house, valleys, and the embankments themselves. Simultaneously, the island begins to coincide with Maitland's own failing, injured body. Having made himself at home in the strangest of landscapes, he is loath to relinquish the shelter of this now-familiar island architecture for the hazards of his former home. Maitland's catharsis resides in this evolving state of desire: to leave all the trappings of his previous life and become one with the island itself. This is the nature of his escape; he ultimately finds inclusion in his state of exile.

> Women have sat indoors all these millions of years, so
> that by this time the very walls are permeated by their
> creative forces.
> —Virginia Woolf, *A Room of One's Own*

To desire (without object) places the autonomy of a desiring subject at risk. A disembodied state of desire is the essence of minoritarian immanence; in architecture, it draws material out of construction, it overrides authorial intentions. It can elicit speech from the very walls that were designed to silence speech. We find such desiring space in Lawrence Thornton's novel *Imagining Argentina*.[23]

Desire is at the heart of protagonist Carlos Rueda's clairvoyant abilities. Family members of *los desaparecidos*[24] come to his courtyard to ask for his for help; Carlos "sees" and tells what has happened to their loved ones. But when his own wife Cecelia and his daughter Teresa are kidnapped, Carlos sees nothing. Meanwhile, in her solitary cell in a prison deep within the Argentine pampas, Cecelia suffers unspeakable acts by prison guards. She has no knowledge of Teresa's whereabouts. Like Jacobo Timerman, she is a journalist by profession; her torment is her lack of paper and pencil, for writing is potentially her means of survival. Unexpectedly, a kind of salvation comes to her through the architecture of her cell:

> One day she sat on her bed staring at the wall on the other
> side of the room. She was so discouraged that her depression
> felt like a physical presence. The walls of her room had been
> plastered by someone who cared for his work and had left
> designs in the plaster, a uniform series of swirling patterns
> from floor to ceiling, from side to side. Cecelia realized that
> the walls offered the answer to her problem. All along she
> had been looking at an index. To each of the patterns she
> could assign paragraphs, starting with the top left-hand side
> of the wall facing her bed. When that wall was filled there
> were the others, and after them she was certain she could
> find ways to make the floor, the windows, even the furniture
> remember for her. By the time she had begun to realize
> something was wrong, that she had not been taken to see
> Teresa for over a month, the walls of her room were filled
> with invisible writing, her words indexed in the swirling
> patterns of a mnemonic system which, when written out,
> would yield hundreds of pages about what she had seen and
> what it means to live in darkness.[25]

As in other prison stories, walls function as an apparatus of exit. But this is not an escape through the wall (as with Timerman and his peephole or Rubashov and the quadratic alphabet). It is not Cecelia who initiates the mechanism; it is that unnamed someone who "cared for his work." Surely the midlevel functionary of the dictatorship that commissioned the prison wanted the construction completed expediently. The patterns in the plaster are not deliberately ornamental; but the plasterer's act of swirling the trowel is significant. It authorizes a latent secret code constructed without any apparent subversive intent. Inscribed onto the wall, this pattern is mere and mute; but once drawn *from* the wall, it has assumed a politicized text.[26]

The text was latent until it was pulled from the wall, read and decoded. The words *read* and *riddle* both come from the Old English *rædan*—"to advise, counsel, guess." Cecelia returns the verb "to read" to its ancient, active sense of deciphering. She extracts words and sentences with deliberate fervor, steals her freedom from the very walls that were designed to take it away. Walls become text, reading becomes writing. The normative convention of transforming writing (or drawing) into built architecture is inverted. Pure materiality becomes a vehicle of escape; and as a journalist, Cecelia's escape is particularly political. It returns us to the "collective value" that is minor architecture's third criterion. Her condition, like that of other prisoners in solitary confinement, approaches Agamben's condition of "bare life" *at the very moment* that her desiring within the plastered walls elevates her from it. Her reading of the room's surfaces is cathartic; but it is also tragic. The message of her daughter's fate is pulled from the wall in a corner of the cell near the floor: "Teresa has been taken away."[27]

The agency of Cecelia's prison wall, heavily inscribed, speaks to that fascinating and elusive phenomenon by which the roles of architecture and architect can be reversed. Her story reveals the unpredictable potential for minor architectures to emerge, long after a work has been designated as complete. Such architectures becomes truly, semantically subjective, which is to say contingent, dependent certainly upon a particular kind of desire yet empty of the desire to possess. Desire in the immediate present projects itself onto seemingly impermeable surfaces.[28] These in turn reflect not the architect (who is only a minor player in the drama) but the immanence of space itself. Cecelia's mnemonic device[29] is connected to memory not in the sense of memorializing an experience or event, but instead as a releasing of the room's own material history, which is then collectively linked to her own need to remember.

> In art, nothing is more secondary than the author's
> intentions.
> —Jorge Luis Borges, "Rudyard Kipling"

Since Vitruvius authored his treatise of ten books, architects have themselves explicitly described and promoted their motivations and intentions. In the Renaissance Alberti, Serlio, and Palladio presented their "books" to the canon; in the early decades of the twentieth century, Le Corbusier published polemics and operative principles for a proprietary new architecture.[30] The CIAM group (Congrès Internationaux d'Architecture Moderne) and others expanded upon the modernist belief in a tabula rasa upon which noble intentions could emerge in pure and ideal form. They advanced principles of function, theorized these at social and civic scales, and articulated methods for their application in the design of modern cities. Following the Second World War, these principles made their way across the Atlantic. Transformed by a more characteristically American agenda, the tenets and intentions of European modernism were prominently applied to social housing developments in service to recently formulated politics and policies of "urban renewal." Central to this agenda was the fervent demolition of what were considered to be blighted blocks and quarters in inner cities, sites upon which publicly funded "projects" were then built.

Of these projects, Pruitt-Igoe in St. Louis was one of the first, and it remains the most notorious. Designed by the Japanese architect Minoru Yamasaki,[31] the complex of thirty-five buildings won a national design award in 1955. But almost from the beginning of its occupation the project was deemed a failure, and in 1971 the city approved its demolition. Historian Charles Jencks has famously cited this event as the definitive end of the modern movement: "Modern Architecture died in St Louis, Missouri on July 15, 1972 at 3:32 p.m. (or thereabouts) when the infamous Pruitt-Igoe scheme, or rather, several of its slab blocks, were given the *coup de grâce* by dynamite."[32] Part of the folklore of Pruitt-Igoe is that it was destroyed by its residents. Though not technically true, tenants registered their frustrations and displeasure with a single voice, spoken in the language of graffiti, vandalism, and neglect. In this instance, collective enunciation reached the ears of the power brokers, who in turn called for wholesale erasure.

In the same year that the first of the Pruitt-Igoe towers was imploded by carefully placed explosives, the Italian architect Mario Fiorentino (a former student of Le Corbusier) began a project of almost identical capacity along the ridge of a hill on the outskirts of Rome. Instead of thirty separate buildings, Corviale is a single kilometer-long structure that forms a veritable wall over thirty meters high between the ancient city and the Tyrrhenian Sea. Its extreme length extends beyond one's cone of sight, compromising the building's identity as a single object. Instead, Corviale may be read as a phenomenal line drawn between two realms and thickened for inhabitation.

The complex took ten years to complete. When it opened in 1982, it housed about eight thousand people and included schools, stores, community spaces, and houses of worship. (Like Ballard's fictional towers, it attempted a certain level of social and economic autonomy.) The lowest level is assigned to parking. Above are several floors of walk-up apartments, above that several more floors of flats. The main public space, according to the original design, was not situated in the conventional center of the plan, but instead was centered in *section*. Between the lower apartments and the upper flats, at approximately the fifth level (the ground level undulates a bit across the topography), was a full floor intended as public and common. The architects and their public client imagined a Corbusian "Main Street" of shops and meeting rooms that would be at the heart of the Corviale community. But the intentions for this space did not adhere; in fact, its public life never materialized at all. No sooner was the building complete and the first apartments occupied than squatters appropriated nearly the full extent of this open level. They arrived with partitioning materials and personal effects, and hastily constructed minor dwellings that soon made "private" space from what had been intended as public.

Over the past three decades in the three- and four-bedroom units on the floors designed for dwelling, children grew up and moved away; now their elderly parents, many of whom are original tenants, sparsely inhabit their furnished rooms. This building that was designed to accommodate over eight thousand residents is now

home to scarcely twenty-five hundred. The fifth floor has nevertheless become increasingly robust—a labyrinthine zone of *favela*-
like informality. Outwardly, by historical definitions and accepted
standards of urbanism, this unplanned colonization represents the
privatization of public space. Yet in the nondialectical realm of
minor architecture, the conventional distinctions between privacy
and publicity are overruled by fluid spatial and social dynamics
that are implicitly but collectively understood.

Some of the tenants' actions have been overtly illegal. Means
of exit are surely not in conformance with building codes, and utilities are pirated from neighbors above and below. Yet though motivated by a spirit of "enterprise," there is an implied and accepted
covenant in this colonization of an intended public zone. On the
floors designed for dwelling, and now so thinly dwelled, there is
surely a sense of missing out on something special, something perhaps too complex, or too subtle, to describe. There is a kind
of pathos, perhaps, engendered through the architectural laws
that lock those residents into their sanctioned spaces, while on
the "free" floor a loose conviviality keeps the distribution of space
in motion. Architects and students visiting Corviale (they now

arrive by busloads) have no access to this level. Collective agreement prohibits it; but this agreement is nowhere written down.[33]

This is one example of a minor architecture taking root at Corviale; another is reflected in the work of the Italian group Stalker. In 2003 these young architects formed an initiative called Osservatorio Nomade, stating as their mission "to rediscover, in the metropolitan territory, a sense that springs from the experience of the present state of things with all its contradictions, from an un-opinionated perspective, free of reassuring and at the same time frustrating historical or functional justifications."[34] Their process is one of walking and talking, remaking space by moving through it, confronting hierarchies and conventions with alternative forms of practice. At Corviale, they engaged the community in a two-year process that became a powerful and nearly immaterial project—a television station operated by and for the Corivale residents.[35] This network of communication operates in real time—a minoritarian force set in motion by the desire to break down the cellular concrete structure of the original building, and accomplished without physically breaking through any walls.[36]

> Where then shall I be brought?
> —Franz Kafka, *Diaries*

Space is the preeminent—and possibly, in our postindustrial economies, the only immediate—material, productive force wherein our social existence is coordinated, set into motion, reproduced, and at times contested. Space, in this way, becomes itself a subject. Particularly in modern fiction, it will often assume the role of a character, even as human "characters" lose their human agency. Kafka's people, more than most, are at the mercy of spatial subjects;[37] they are predictable and repetitive even in name (Josef K., K., Karl). Kafka describes actions rather than appearances; he organizes by distance rather than location. Words and gestures spatialize rather than moralize.[38] Exchanges are strangely symmetrical, as in the relationship between K. and Barnabas in *The Castle*. Kafka's subjects, stripped of subjectivity, become mere loci, intersections in a spatial network that folds back on itself not only within each story but from story to story and novel to novel. This instrumentality has no tangible outcome. Nothing happens.[39] Nothing begins and nothing ends, either in the historical frame of time or in the geographical frame of space. Kafka's people are always diminishing toward becoming animals or machines.

Benjamin paraphrases Kafka: "'There is an infinite amount of hope, but not for us.' . . . This is the source of [Kafka's] radiant serenity."[40] Deleuze and Guattari also refer to Kafka's writing as "joyous."[41] It is clearly not a typical joy that emanates from his human characters (though the animals often hum or break out in song). Benjamin emphasizes Kafka's failure, but failure here is redefined.[42] The messenger who fails to deliver the message affirms a certain kind of space, one elongated, multiplied, and juxtaposed upon (and against) all expectations. Failure is an affirmation of immanence, of a radiance just out of reach. Who can say what narratives the walls of Pruitt-Igoe might have written, had they been given time and space?

Ahab, pursuing his nemesis, the object of his great obsession, questions his own subjectivity, casts himself as a generic everyman; he is one, but acting for all. In the oceanic city that is not open like the ocean, a multiplicity of architects pursue a small number of "white whales," then an even smaller number of awards and opportunities for publication. Worth is quantified—numbers of clients, "projects in the pipeline," pictures in journals. With all this emphasis on recognition, wherein lies the incentive to be anonymous? Who will capitalize a minor project, or authorize permission to occupy the vacant spaces so recently produced by (that other) capital's failed agendas? How does an architect *become* minor? What ambitions must be

dismantled and what expectations let go? Perhaps most importantly, what is put at risk? The biggest risk is surely the risk or even the certainty of failure, for while success is framed by constructions that persist through time and have achieved notoriety, works of minor architecture are defined by their refusal to conform to these expectations. These works rarely have patrons. By definition, they never reach completion.

Let us once again look to Benjamin's destructive character, who

> sees nothing permanent. But for this very reason he sees
> ways everywhere. Where others encounter walls or moun-
> tains, there, too, he sees a way. But because he sees a way
> everywhere, he has to clear things from it everywhere. Not
> always by brute force; sometimes by the most refined.
> Because he sees ways everywhere, he always stands at a
> crossroads. No moment can know what the next will bring.
> What exists he reduces to rubble—not for the sake of
> rubble, but for that of the way leading through it.[43]

A minor architect is a minor destructive character, a tinkerer and hacker, journalist and editor, alter ego and subaltern. But tinkerers may sabotage as well as fix, and willfully take apart rather than assemble. Hackers may scramble code as often as decipher it, and editors (to save us from our wordiness) ruthlessly slice the excess away. Were he to tend toward a minor architecture, Valéry's Eupalinos might choose to say: "By dint of deconstructing, I truly believe that I have deconstructed myself."

Interiors proliferate outward; they escape. Objects proliferate in place; they fragment. For the architect/subject, to become minor is to exchange focused ambition for scattered flight and love of masters for that rejection of master languages with which we began.

THE MYTH OF NATURE

Substance is eternal.
—Lucretius, *De rerum natura*

But these are all landsmen; of weekdays pent up in lath
and plaster—tied to counters, nailed to benches, clinched
to desks. How then is this? Are the green fields gone?
What do they here?
—Herman Melville, *Moby Dick*

Mythologized nature is now architecture's most precious commodity, canonized and invested with messianic powers. As a code of conduct, allegiance to the myth of nature has permeated every crevice of media culture, overtaken the sanctions of practice, and addressed itself to the alleviation of our collective guilt. At the same time, the illusion that emerging technologies will recalibrate our relationship with nature, and that architecture can be their handmaiden, holds us in thrall. Yet much like the object and subject myths discussed in previous chapters, these current guises of nature mask a set of practices and products that defer to the hegemony of capital, and continue to support our highly stratified, postindustrial economy.

Historically, nature has been cast as an enigmatic "other." But primordial nature as that which preceded (and precedes) civilization and culture is necessarily mythic; it disappeared at the very moment that it became so explicitly defined. Positioned in opposition to culture, the concept of nature is itself a cultural invention—constructed around the vicissitudes of human history alternately as antagonist or ally, as a subject of fear or of pathos, cast into exile or placed in protective custody.[1] Nature's place in the discipline of architecture is particularly striking: it is both celebrated and excluded. The acanthus leaves of a Corinthian column and Peter Zumthor's wet stone walls celebrate nature; caulking applied to windows and levees constructed around delta cities are intended to exclude nature's most powerful forces. The floods of Hurricane Katrina forced a massive exodus from New Orleans, a deterritorialization accompanied by a reterritorialization *by the flood waters themselves*. "Yea, foolish mortals," Melville cautioned, "Noah's flood is not yet subsided,"[2] and years after the storm the question persists: do we reclaim New Orleans from the Gulf waters once again, or retreat to higher ground? In anticipation of ongoing climate change and the inevitability of rising water, one of the great debates is whether to include or to exclude—to periodically recalibrate our plans for harbor cities as the ice caps continue to melt, or to preempt the effects of the flood with engineered barriers against rising tides.

"Yet this great flux is made of all such things as you have
known or might have known. This vast irregular sheet
of water, which rushes by without respite, rolls all colors
toward nothingness. See how dim it all is."
—Paul Valéry, "Eupalinos, or the Architect"

These are the waters of the mythic river Ilissus. Here Valéry places Socrates and Phaedrus, their dialogue adhering to strict Platonic form, but their ephemeral selves transported by literary license to the afterworld of the early twentieth century.[3] Mere shades in death, and with all eternity before them, they meet in that dim landscape where "nothing is clear." Phaedrus introduces the subject of architecture through his remembrances of an architect named Eupalinos,[4] whose precepts become the provocation for an extended debate on the distinctions between *constructing* and *knowing*. We soon discover that Socrates' fascination with these questions is not merely academic. In that realm where ideas flow freely without the support of substance, he expresses some regret for his mortal life of pure thought, and wonders how he might have contributed as an architect.[5]

At the close of the dialogue, Socrates delivers a tour de force soliloquy in which he casts himself as "the Anti-Socrates" and imagines himself in the role of "the Constructor." He begins by describing the circumstances before God intervened:

> Note, Phaedrus, that when the Demiurge set about making the world, he grappled with the confusion of Chaos. All formlessness spread before him. Nor could he find a single handful of matter, in all this waste, that was not infinitely impure and composed of an infinity of substances.

Here is the quintessence of Deleuzian smoothness. Socrates continues:

> He valiantly came to grips with this frightful mixture of dry and wet, of hard and soft, of light and gloom that made up this chaos, whose disorder penetrated into its smallest parts. He disentangled that faintly luminous mud, of which not a single particle was pure, and wherein all energies were diluted, so that the past and the future, accident and substance, the lasting and the fleeting, propinquity and remoteness, motion and rest, the light and the heavy were as completely mingled as wine with water, when poured into one cup. The Great Shaper was the enemy of similitudes

and of those hidden identities that we delight to come upon. He organized inequality. . . . He divided the hot from the cold and the evening from the morning; He squeezed out from the mud the sparkling seas and pure waters, lifting the mountains out of the waves, and portioning out in fair islands whatever concreteness remained.

The world is organized, stratified. That original "nature" created by the demiurge is defined by its segmented quality—materials and binary attributes separated and in opposition. Socrates describes an orderly yard of building materials, ready and desiring to be set in motion again. He has set the stage for the art of architecture to begin:

But the Constructor whom I am now bringing to the fore finds before him, as his chaos and primitive matter, precisely that world order which the Demiurge wrung from the disorder of the beginning. Nature is formed, and the elements are separated; but something enjoins him to consider this work as unfinished. . . . He takes as his starting point of this act, the very point where the god had left off. —In the beginning, he says to himself, there was what is: the mountains and forests; the deposits and veins; red clay, yellow sand, and the white stone which will give us lime.[6]

Architecture has evolved as the art of putting things together, of collage and montage and of making assemblages. In the beginning it was stone upon stone, primitive assemblages of a single material. Eventually, ornament and color were applied to tell stories that brought elements of nature into a deliberate, cultural narrative. Builders still worked this reciprocity between nature and culture at the time that Valéry wrote his dialogue. But as we have continued to build more (and more) buildings, more (and more) separate products have been brought into play. With each advance in product development (also thoroughly profit-driven), architectural details have involved greater numbers of materials and things. Within every building, proliferating layers of construction employ their separate syntaxes. This language has become heavy with modifiers and clauses, overwrought with the implications of competing aesthetic and functional decisions. These complex grammars are the thinly veiled relations of a competitive marketplace.

Our challenge is to deterritorialize and reterritorialize, to engage the minor mode within these complicated, oversaturated assemblages, and to approach that point where "language stops being representative in order to move toward its extremities or its limits."[7] In order for us to do this, a complicated building must be made to reveal its simple, "natural" form.

> There are peregrine falcons uptown, downtown and
> midtown. They zoom through the canyons of Wall Street
> and perch on the gargoyles of Riverside Church.
> —*New York Times*, June 15, 1995

In 1972, only a few peregrine falcons existed east of the Mississippi River, and none in the west.[8] Our pervasive use of DDT had caused the chemical to seep into the birds' habitats and hence into their food supply, causing eggshells to thin and crack before hatching. When wildlife biologists proposed transplanting the few remaining birds to high-rise buildings in urban centers, where the food supply (mostly pigeons) would be free of pesticides, their plan was greeted with skepticism. Yet over the course of the next two decades, more than fifty cities in the United States and Canada eventually participated in the program, depositing pairs of birds (the falcon mates for life) on such clifflike promontories as the Brooklyn Bridge in New York, Toronto's Sheraton Hotel, and the Fisher Building in Detroit. In 1992, with over nine hundred pairs counted, the peregrine falcon was removed from the national endangered species list.

If we did not know better, we might think that the falcons had appropriated our colloquialisms of urban canyon and urban jungle for their own purpose. But the falcon's reading of this urban landscape is literal, not metaphorical. World cities of commerce are formed by clusters of tall and densely packed buildings, built topographies that echo the natural cliffs, canyons, and plateaus that form the falcons' indigenous habitats, where they can dive at speeds of up to 200 miles per hour for their prey. These raptors responded without prejudice or preconceptions to the *physical* conditions of vertical distance and craggy footholds; they perceived the simple forms. Their responsiveness to what all assumed would be an alien landscape has much to teach us about how to redefine "nature" in the context of the contemporary metropolis.

The falcon introduces porosity into the city—not the shadowy porosity of Benjamin's Naples, but instead a city shot through with wildness, a city reducing its mass by introducing small pockets of decidedly nonhuman use. Animals operate according to their own time frame, and the nesting box on the roof of the PG&E building in San Francisco sat empty for seventeen seasons before being discovered and claimed by a falcon pair in 2003. Since then, a web cam has entertained us with the daily urban life of falcon parents George and Gracie and their yearly offspring.[9]

Driven from their habitat, driven to the brink of extinction, the falcons' transplantation to the city is a reterritorialization of the first order.[10] Reterritorialization erases property lines and other abstract geometries; it introduces mobility and blurs urban segments into newly integrated ecologies. And remarkably, neither falcons nor humans need deterritorialize one another. For us as for the falcon, the constructed city can take on a palpable and primal existence, empty of symbols, meaning, history, and memory. To engage the practice of minor architecture is to reterritorialize by first partly forgetting those values firmly affixed to provenance (history) and to preservation (materiality). In the case of the falcons, the anthropomorphic and anthropocentric interests that have historically defined the function of the city itself are partly relaxed; the intellect of urbanism as a discipline embraces its sensual, better half.

In a story by Anita Desai,[11] a sick man named Basu is suffering from the stifling heat of his apartment bedroom. He asks his wife to bring his mattress up onto the roof of their building. The bedroom is deterritorialized, the roof reterritorialized. Under the stars, he gets his first good sleep in weeks. As day begins to break, he delights in the view of pigeons silhouetted against the morning light. Basu leaves his stuffy bedroom; the falcon leaves the contaminated mountains. Though they approach from opposite directions, each finds a certain wild territory on an urban rooftop. In both cases, reterritorialization is an exit to the outside.

Architecture is a collection of ruins that closes at six o'clock.
—Jennifer Bloomer and Robert Segrest, "Without
Architecture"

Ruins are the evidence of things become obsolete, projects halted, capital exhausted. It is no longer simply the collapse of a building that makes it a ruin; it is the collapse of a symbolic order. How sad that architecture (the "useful" art) becomes the physical, visible manifestation of that which is no longer useful.

In the second half of the twentieth century, the abandoned buildings of obsolete industries, tough high-ceilinged spaces once the sites of blue-collar work, were quite suddenly romanced and coveted as living spaces for an urban gentry. More recently, unfinished highrise towers in Bangkok, Shanghai, and Caracas have attracted the attention of bloggers and photographers as vivid "follies" of globalization. The more banal (and completed) buildings of the neoliberal economy have yet to receive much similar attention; but in 2003 the pathos of dead and dying malls attracted the interest of a group in Los Angeles, who sponsored a national competition inviting architects to speculate on the malls' physical and cultural futures.[12] Even more recently, the six thousand Circuit City retail stores that were closed in 2009 became the site for a collaborative thesis project in the Department of Architecture at the University of California, Berkeley.[13]

These are but a few of many possible contexts for minor architectures, settings not so much for salvage operations as for nearly authorless insurgencies. As an archaeology without artifacts, the process of spatial reclamation is more low-tech than high, and privileges the passions of labor over the physics of materials. At the same time, other forces may be brought into play—forces of weather, systems of drainage, even migration patterns of birds. These may yield new concepts for workplaces not so "pent up in lath and plaster," more open to outside air and with more connections between buildings—opportunities to make architecture less stable and more porous. These practices may produce unlikely juxtapositions, assemblages of spaces rather than of things. Of course such transformations already exist. They are mostly undocumented—this too is in the nature of the minor mode. But some, like the circulation system through the downtown buildings of Minneapolis that allow one to navigate the city above ground and indoors in the cold months, are well known as innovative urban infrastructure. (In Houston, there is instead a subterranean network that provides respite from the sweltering heat.)

The Michigan Theater in Detroit, constructed in 1926 on the site of the workshop where Henry Ford built his first car, closed its doors and was partially demolished in 1967, then repurposed as a parking garage in 1982. (Ironically, the demise of the old theater is sometimes attributed to a lack of parking.) Unlike the gentrification of

former industrial spaces, this is an example of a prosaic use moving into a space originally designed for more elite cultural functions. Tattered velvet curtains frame a ruined stage, which is merely a backdrop for vehicles casually parked where an audience once sat. The resulting spectacular aesthetic gives the theater its iconic stature as an example of adaptive reuse.

> Half-ruined buildings once again take on
> The look of buildings waiting to be finished.
> —Bertolt Brecht, "Of All the Works of Man"

For fifteen years the ghostly half-finished (half-ruined) Torre de David loomed vacantly over the city of Caracas, Venezuela. The tower was begun in 1990, then abandoned when its patron died unexpectedly. (Its name sounds biblical, but it ironically and unofficially refers to financier and speculator David Brillembourg.) At forty-five stories the tower is one of the tallest buildings in Latin America. It has no working elevators, and no connection to urban utility systems. Several years ago its open floors beckoned to the homeless population of Caracas, and now over 2,500 people live there.[14] Squatters sleep in spaces that were intended to be executive corner offices; some climb as many as twenty-six floors each day. If we squint, the Torre de David becomes a kind of cliff dwelling—where people, like falcons, have recognized the accommodating potential of a vertical urban structure, and taken advantage of its accidental ecology.

The settlement of the tower, like that of more conventional ground-based urban *favelas*, has happened over time. The first group of three hundred pioneers sought shelter from the streets in 2007: "'The night we came in, I was scared, but I was also excited to finally have my own home,' says Jhonny Jimenez."[15] He is a member of the founding group, and is now one of the tower's main social and maintenance coordinators. The building functions as a nearly autonomous urban settlement, with volunteers organizing health services, security, and recreation. People pay a small monthly fee for improvements, which include spaces for child care and a church currently under construction. "Corner" shops are staggered vertically throughout the inhabited floors, and informal live-work arrangements include hair salons and cafes. Water and waste are carried up and down by hand, but civil courtesies prevail. The elderly are given the floors closest to the ground, and larger families are awarded larger amounts of space.

On the partially completed but inaccessible roof, a helicopter landing pad reminds us of corporate ambitions gone awry. Had the tower been finished as planned, it would be silent and complicit— cocooned in acoustical layers of carpets and ceilings, and thermal layers of insulation and glass. Some of the people who are now living and sleeping there might instead be employed on the night cleaning crew. Given the market's decline over the past several years, they would likely be working in a building considerably empty of tenants.

But the availability of this real estate skeleton announced itself more publicly than vacancies within completed structures—a scaffold without skin, presumed empty of function. The tower's half-finished state, halfway to ruin, available for deconstruction, preempted the need for demolition. Meanwhile, the circumstantial geometry of its half-finished state and the ensuing ad hoc development in its density have destroyed all intended symmetries of the original design. The once silent floors have come to life, and robust family activity is exposed to the city as transparently as in a painting by Ralph Fassanella. This recent settlement in Caracas has marked similarities to the informal fifth floor of Corviale, but raised to a higher power. It is even more aggressively minor and surely has the promise of an even shorter life.

Since the language is arid, make it vibrate with a new intensity.
—Gilles Deleuze and Felix Guattari, *Kafka*

The dross landscapes of our metropolitan hinterlands are approaching a field of consistency. Already we have seen the wasted margins of the postindustrial landscape become strange attractors. Sites blighted by poisoned soil and vandalized buildings still with the industrial charm of steel sash divided-lite windows are reclaimed as enclaves of an alternative, progressive culture. But more recently constructed buildings (much maligned for their lack of "character") remain stubbornly mute; only the empty parking lots and the estate agents' bold signage give evidence of their increasing vacancies. Their silence is part of the reason we profess to find them so objectionable. They are content and ubiquitous; in appearance they refuse to acknowledge regional styles, climates, or landscapes. Most would prefer to think that these "developer" buildings are not truly Architecture at all (in its most profound, or at least conventional, academic sense). They are not special, they have no provenance. And this is our opportunity: without the anxieties that often accompany architectural transformation, their arid language can be deconstructed and diminished toward language without meaning. (The lush language of classicism has long outlived its ability to propagate, though architectural historians will rightly argue that buildings of the past continue to communicate.) The perceived poverty of these buildings releases us from responsibility to adhere to any laws, covenants, or precedents. This is precisely what makes them vulnerable to minor experiments, and valuable as another kind of "natural" resource. Open to new intensities, these graveyards of capital are the fields, forests, and quarries of our present time.

As J. G. Ballard might have asked, "Why could people not fall in love with the airport Hilton, when they were falling in love with the Louvre all the time?"[16] The buildings we have been referring to (a genre that includes the Hilton) are the products of politics delivered from above. But once realized, they may forfeit the abstractions of finance, hierarchy, ambition, and all the interior object and subject myths we have embedded within them. Ballard's question is not simply rhetorical (though our affection for these buildings may take a different, perhaps ironic form from the aesthetic passions of former times). We are perhaps moving toward an image of how a politics from below might be mobilized within the banal spaces of an airport hotel. Let us reflect upon several conditions that we have already identified—an empty, sealed interior; an object afloat in an arid sea of asphalt; an as-yet-unformed collective that might include a public official, an owner with an unproductive asset, an architect with an adventurous spirit and an open mind. Our starting point is the order and constructed matter of the civilized world. Like the original nature that Valéry's original architect found so unfinished, we see these sites again as a point of departure. We perceive in them latent lines of force, states of incompleteness, things desiring to be taken apart—freed from master languages, all that those languages imply, and the little they allow. Every word, every building lends itself to excavation—not just to discover its formal past, but to exit toward its less formal future.

We have cycled around to a place where the image of the city-as-nature emerges with a sense of urgency. An omega moment returns us to an alpha condition; nature and culture approach each other in a blurred reciprocity that rejects the false and destructive distinctions between them. "'Here I am, says the Constructor, I am the act.'"[17]

But were Valéry writing today,[18] Socrates might become a mere and vague embodiment of the *deconstructor*. He might instead say:

> *The minor architects whom we are now bringing to the fore find before them, as their chaos and primitive matter, precisely that order which the Architects wrung from the disorder of nature. Architecture is formed, and the elements are joined in complex assemblages. Details and intricate hardware, caulks and sealants of refined chemistry and varieties of glass in their unbelievably thin titanium frames—all this seems at first complete; but something enjoins them to consider this work as unfinished, as required to be set in motion again. They take as the starting point of their act the very point where the Architect left off: "We will begin with what is: the buildings and streets, abandoned factories, unfinished towers, highways in lines and loops that slice through cities and carve the once-fluid landscape into segments, malls and megastores in their vast seas of asphalt. In the cities, office towers with too little purpose and too much space; in the suburbs, wasted interior acreages of foreclosed homes and office buildings barely finished before the IPOs collapsed." All this they see as available.*

Here is an infinite amount of hope, even for us. So much space is available!—an embarrassment of riches disguised in mediocrity. What is ubiquitous is also latent with specific desires. Every city has its deep ecology, its geometries of vacancy, inventories of waste, politics of space and consequent lines of flight. The same Indo-European root that gave us the relationship between "door" and "forest" is also the root of "foreclosure"—a contemporary phenomenon engendered through the economic abstractions of development dislocated from material history. The resulting vacancies are already out of balance, space is pressed out the door, listing toward the outside. Like a book no one is reading,[19] a vacant building vibrates with unseen intensities, ready to shed its excess, its burden of overwrought grammars, its syntax of profitability: its closed interior and its brittle shell. If we can, let us imagine emptiness recalibrated, space unfolded toward smooth and slippery and nonconforming use. American cities, in particular, are full of overstuffed assemblages waiting to be unpacked.

So we return to the premise with which we began: minor architectures will emerge through (and as) the substance of architecture. This is their nature.

Like many books, this one started out with a longer and even more eclectic narrative. The editorial process consigned many fragments not to the trashcan but to this extensive section of notes. Their order and adjacencies may in places seem as random as the tombstones in the Old Jewish Cemetery in Prague, where as many as twelve layers of graves and over 12,000 stones are crowded into a relatively small urban site. In both these contexts hierarchies are flattened, contingencies celebrated, major figures reduced to a minor voice.

PREFACE

Epigraph   *The Complete Lyrics of Cole Porter*, ed. Robert Kimball (New York: Knopf, 1983), 362. (Lyrics from "Ev'ry Time We Say Goodbye" originally published by Chappell & Company, 1944.) Notable is Porter's clever use of parallel construction: as the lyrics "There is no love song finer / But how strange the change / From major to minor / Ev'ry time we say goodbye" are sung, the song literally changes its tonality from major to minor mode.

1. William H. Gass, "Invisible Cities," *Via* 7 (University of Pennsylvania, 1984); reprinted in his *Tests of Time: Essays* (Chicago: University of Chicago Press, 2002), 41.

2. Indra McEwen, *Socrates' Ancestor* (Cambridge: MIT Press, 1992).

3. Jennifer Bloomer, *Architecture and the Text: The (S)crypts of Joyce and Piranesi* (New Haven: Yale University Press, 1993), 174. Bloomer began an exploration of "a minor architecture" in design

studios she taught at Georgia Tech (1986–1988), the University of Florida (1988–1991), and Iowa State University (1992–1994). "Supplementing the Sites of Practice: Towards a Minor Architecture" was the subject of her 1992 Annual Discourse to the Royal Institute of British Architects.

Janet McCaw used Bloomer's proposition of minor architecture (and her work on James Joyce) as a point of departure for an essay titled "Architectural (S)crypts: In Search of a Minor Architecture," *Architectural Theory Review* 4, no. 1 (1999), in which she addresses the installation art of Tadashi Kawamata.

I WHAT IS A MINOR ARCHITECTURE?

Epigraph All quotations from *Moby Dick* are taken from Herman Melville, *Moby Dick* (London: J. M. Dent and Sons, 1977).

1. Manfredo Tafuri, in *Theories and Histories of Architecture*, refers to "major" architectures as repositories of meaning. The term is contextualized within a discussion of pavilions that "allude to something other than themselves." Cited in Jennifer Bloomer, *Architecture and the Text: The (S)crypts of Joyce and Piranesi* (New Haven: Yale University Press, 1993), 41.

2. The first reference is to the Michigan Theater in Detroit, the second to the Torre de David in Caracas. Each of these is discussed further in chapter V.

3. "Multiplicity" is a philosophical concept developed by Edmund Husserl and Henri Bergson, in response to Georg Riemann's mathematics. The idea of multiplicity is central to the theories of Deleuze and Guattari, who define its essence as a matter of *subtraction* rather than of addition. "The multiple must be made, not by always adding a higher dimension, but rather in the simplest of ways, by dint of sobriety, with the number of dimensions one already has available—always $N - 1$. Subtract the unique

from the multiplicity to be constituted; write (we would say 'design') at $N - 1$ dimensions." Gilles Deleuze and Félix Guattari, *A Thousand Plateaus: Capitalism and Schizophrenia*, trans. Brian Massumi (Minneapolis: University of Minnesota Press, 1987), 6.

4. As early as 1934 Walter Benjamin wrote: "There are two ways to miss the point in Kafka's works. One is to interpret them naturally; the other is the supernatural interpretation. Both the psychoanalytic and the theological interpretations equally miss the essential points." Benjamin, "Franz Kafka," in *Illuminations*, ed. Hannah Arendt, trans. Harry Zohn (New York: Schocken Books, 1969). Like Benjamin, Deleuze and Guattari firmly resist the kinds of metaphysical and symbolic readings that characterize most Kafka criticism.

5. As an example, they point to the films of Jean-Luc Godard, which evince "a strange poverty that makes French a minor language within French." Gilles Deleuze and Félix Guattari, *Kafka: Toward a Minor Literature* (Minneapolis: University of Minnesota Press, 1991), 23.

6. See note 12 of chapter III.

7. "The first characteristic of minor literature . . . is that in it language is affected with a high coefficient of deterritorialization. . . . The second characteristic of minor literatures is that everything in them is political. . . . The third characteristic of minor literature is that in it everything takes on a collective value." Deleuze and Guattari, *Kafka*, 16–17. The first of these qualities is particularly attributable to Deleuze and Guattari. They develop the concept of "deterritorialization" in *Anti-Oedipus* (1972), in the context of labor power freed from a specific means of production. More generally, deterritorialization can describe any process that removes a set of relations from their normal context, rendering them virtual and immanent. It is in this sense that they apply the

term to Kafka's writing. In *A Thousand Plateaus* (1980), they distinguish between relative and absolute deterritorialization. Relative deterritorialization is always accompanied by reterritorialization, while positive, absolute deterritorialization implies an unappropriated "plane of immanence." In developing an approach to the practice of minor architecture, I am blurring the boundary between relative and absolute forms. While peregrine falcons (see chapter V) may claim office towers for their site of recovery, this claim is not absolute; the reterritorialization leaves open the potential to itself be deterritorialized. The sites remain immanent.

8. Jorge Luis Borges once referred obliquely to the impoverishment of Kafka's fiction: "Perhaps the strength of Kafka may lie in his lack of complexity." This is in the context of comparing Kafka to Henry James. Richard Burgin, *Conversations with Jorge Luis Borges* (New York: Avon, 1968), 76.

9. According to Henri Lefebvre, "There is a politics of space, because space is political." Lefebvre, "Reflections on the Politics of Space," *Antipode Journal* 8, no. 2 (1976), 33.

10. Throughout most of this book I have chosen to capitalize the word "State," in order to emphasize its role as a dominant structure of power—implying personification, and metaphorically an individual, "proper" authority.

11. Carl Schmitt reflects on this ambiguity: "One seldom finds a clear definition of the political. The word is most frequently used negatively, in contrast to various other ideas, for example in such antitheses as politics and economy, politics and morality, politics and law; and within law there is again politics and civil law, and so forth. By means of such negative, often also polemical confrontations, it is usually possible, depending upon the context and concrete situation, to characterize something with clarity. But this is still not a specific definition. In one way or another 'political' is generally juxtaposed to 'state' or at least is brought

into relation with it. The state thus appears as something political, the political as something pertaining to the state—obviously an unsatisfactory circle." Carl Schmitt, *The Concept of the Political* (Chicago: University of Chicago Press, 1996), 20.

12. In typical Situationist exuberance (and self-importance), Guy Debord wrote in 1964, "While contemporary impotence blathers on about the belated project of 'getting into the twentieth century,' we think it is high time to eliminate the dead time that has dominated this century. . . . Here as elsewhere, the road of excess leads to the palace of wisdom. Ours is the best effort so far toward getting out of the 20th century." In Ken Knabb, ed., *Situationist International Anthology* (Berkeley: Bureau of Public Secrets, 1995), 138.

13. All references to Bataille's writing on architecture are from Denis Hollier, *Against Architecture* (Cambridge: MIT Press, 1992).

14. Robert Harris's novel *Fatherland*, an "alternative" historical fiction based on the hypothesis of a German victory in World War II, provides an image of State-sponsored architecture in Berlin as is might have developed had the Reich continued its regime. In the words of a tour guide: "The Great Hall is the largest building in the world. It rises to a height of more than a quarter of a kilometer, and on certain days—observe today—the top of the dome is lost from view. The dome itself is one hundred and forty meters in diameter, and St. Peter's in Rome will fit into it sixteen times. . . . The Great Hall is used only for the most solemn ceremonies of the German Reich and has a capacity of one hundred and eighty thousand people. One interesting and unforeseen phenomenon: the breath from this number of humans rises into the cupola and forms clouds, which condense and fall as light rain. The Great Hall is the only building in the world that generates its own climate." Robert Harris, *Fatherland* (London: Hutchinson, 1992), 24.

15. Hollier, *Against Architecture*, 46–47.

16. See Deleuze and Guattari, *A Thousand Plateaus*, 371. Chapter 10, "1440: The Smooth and the Striated," is devoted to an analysis of these two spatial qualities, and the complex ways in which they overlap, intersect, and morph into one another.

17. Throughout this book, "desire" is used in the sense set forth by Félix Guattari in *Soft Subversions*, ed. Sylvère Lotringer (New York: Semiotext(e), 1996), 273. "Desire is the fact that in a closed world, a process arises that secretes other systems of reference, which authorize, although nothing is ever guaranteed, the opening of new degrees of freedom."

18. For example, in the story "The Burrow" Kafka's ubiquitous animal is obsessed with a major task of constructing its underground house. The work is never completed; neither does it afford an escape route. Instead, every line leads back to the insidious interior, the Castle Keep.

19. Franz Kafka, "Two Introductory Parables," in *The Complete Stories*, ed. Nahum N. Glazer (New York: Schocken Books, 1946), 3–5.

20. Kafka describes this event as a segmented process, with gangs of workers building a length of wall before then being shifted to a new location. It is what he calls a "principle of piecemeal construction. . . . In fact it is said that there are gaps [in the wall] that have never been filled in at all." Franz Kafka, "The Great Wall of China," in *The Complete Stories*, 238.

21. Benjamin spent more than ten years in the Bibliothèque Nationale in Paris compiling literary and philosophical fragments that form a composite study of material and spatial culture, an encyclopedic narrative of nineteenth-century Paris. When the Nazi army occupied Paris in 1940 Benjamin was forced to flee southward to the Spanish border; he entrusted the thousands of notes to Georges Bataille, who hid them in the Bibliothèque. In the 1980s the edited manuscript was published in German as *Passagenwerk*, and in English in 1999 as *The Arcades Project*, trans.

Howard Eiland and Kevin McLaughlin (Cambridge: Belknap Press of Harvard University Press, 1999).

22. This genre of contemporary fiction is the focus of Annie Dillard's *Living by Fiction* (New York: Harper Colophon, 1982).

23. More often quoted is the line, "Those books of stone, so solid and so durable, would give way to the book of paper, even more solid and more durable." Victor Hugo, *The Hunchback of Notre Dame*, trans. John Sturrock (New York: Penguin, 1978), chapter 1.

Ray Bradbury's dystopian novel *Fahrenheit 451* presents both books and buildings at their most vulnerable—books are burned and buildings are bombed. But in the final scene, particularly in the film version of the story, a form of collective enunciation reconstructs both stories and spaces, as the intellectual survivors of a fascist regime develop space through walking, and remember texts through recitation. See the image from the film on page 70.

24. For the most complete discussion and analysis of this shift in economic/political structure, see Fredric Jameson, *Postmodernism, or, the Cultural Logic of Late Capitalism* (Durham: Duke University Press, 1991).

25. Karl Marx, in *The Marx-Engels Reader* (New York: Norton, 1978), 577–578.

Epigraph Joseph Raphson, a lesser-known mathematician, constructed a set of axioms about space, of which this is the fourth. The passage as quoted is from Alexandre Koyré, *From the Closed World to the Infinite Universe* (Baltimore: Johns Hopkins University Press, 1968), 195. Koyré emphasizes the fact that Raphson considered space as *substance*, in contrast to the formulations of Henry More, which cast space as *spirit*.

26. Walter Benjamin, "The Destructive Character," in *Reflections: Essays, Aphorisms, Autobiographical Writings*, ed. Peter Demetz,

trans. Edmund Jephcott (New York: Harcourt Brace Jovanovich, 1978), 301.

27. In the seventeenth century, the words *experiment* and *experience* were synonyms, descending alike from the Latin *experiri,* "to try," and ultimately from the Indo-European root **per,* meaning "to risk." Minor architectures are experiments with the *active* experience of space—and they necessarily involve risk.

28. The competing claims of Leibniz and Newton for the invention of calculus are well known and still debated. Their theories differ with respect to how the science of limits relates to space. For Leibniz, space is a lattice of quantitative relations; for Newton, it is a unity that precedes relationships. Dirk Struik discusses Leibniz's calculus as integral to his conceptual pursuit of the infinite and the abstract, in contrast to Newton's more functional approach. Struik, *A Concise History of Mathematics* (New York: Dover, 1948).

29. Michel de Certeau, *The Practice of Everyday Life,* trans. Steven Rendall (Berkeley: University of California Press, 1988), 117. De Certeau's use of the words "space" and "place" is semantically opposite that of the Dutch architect Aldo van Eyck, who often said: "Whatever Space and Time mean, Place and Occasion mean more. For Space in the image of man is Place, and Time in the image of man is Occasion."

30. Manfredo Tafuri, *Architecture and Utopia: Design and Capitalist Development,* trans. Barbara Luigia La Penta (Cambridge: MIT Press, 1976), 182.

31. See Guy Davenport, "Making It Uglier to the Airport," in *Every Force Evolves a Form* (San Francisco: North Point Press, 1987), 156–165. The title of the essay is taken from Louis Zukofsky's poem "'A'-18": "all / their world's done to change the world is / to make it more ugly to the airport." Davenport's essay explores the relationship between the forces of capital, intent on profit

through development, and the power of a local community (though unnamed, it is Bolinas, California) to resist this force.

32. ". . . still unknown sounds that come from the near future—Fascism, Stalinism, Americanism, *diabolical powers that are knocking at the door.*" Deleuze and Guattari, *Kafka*, 41.

II   THE MYTH OF THE INTERIOR

Epigraph   The eight blue octavo notebooks discovered by Max Brod among Kafka's papers span the years 1917–1919, a period during which Kafka had stopped writing in his diary. They are smaller than the quarto notebooks that hold the diaries, and are less personal—mostly philosophical fragments, aphorisms, and ideas for stories. They do, however, contain numerous references to Kafka's ongoing illness; some days have only the two-word entry "In bed." Franz Kafka, *The Blue Octavo Notebooks*, trans. Ernst Kaiser and Eithne Wilkins (Cambridge, Mass.: Exact Change, 1991).

1. Henri Blanchot argues that Kafka's exclusion from the quotidian aspects of life, most pronounced during his illnesses, trapped him within an interior marked by the absence of circumstances conducive to writing. "When one has all one's time, one no longer has time, and 'favorable' exterior circumstances have become the—unfavorable—fact that there are no longer any circumstances." Henri Blanchot, *The Space of Literature*, trans. Ann Smock (Lincoln: University of Nebraska Press, 1982), 60.

2. For Lefebvre the preeminent quality of the political is permanence or "the eternal"—I am considering this as the interior of time, a condition engendered by "politics from above." See Henri Lefebvre, *The Production of Space*, trans. Donald Nicholson-Smith (Oxford: Blackwell, 1991), 95.

3. The painter Titorelli explains to Josef K. that there exist three potential directions for the legal unfolding of his case: indefinite postponement, ostensible acquittal, and definite acquittal. Of

course K. hopes for the last. But when he challenges the painter further, Titorelli goes to great lengths to explain that both ostensible acquittal and definite acquittal are subject to insurmountable tautological contradictions, and hence are impossible after all. The only possible outcome, then, is "indefinite postponement." This is one of the indications that perhaps the end of the novel as published—K.'s execution "like a dog"—is not what the author intended. (See note 5 below.)

Epigraph The English word *window* replaced the Old English words *eagþyrl*, literally "eye-hole," and *eagduru*, "eye-door," both of which semantically privileged view over ventilation. The modern word originates from the Old Norse *vindauga* from *vindr*, "wind," and *auga*, "eye," transforming the meaning from an aperture for view to one for wind. Its first recorded use in English, ironically, refers to a hole in the roof of a shed, unglazed and presumably only for ventilation. Technically, Titorelli's skylight is neither a window (eye for the wind) nor an *eagduru* (door for the eye), though his door, with its loose boards that permit the girls to peer through, is certainly the latter.

    The current language of architectural contract documents still adheres to the original meaning of window—which is defined by its ability to open for ventilation. The technical term for Titorelli's skylight is "fixed glazing."

4. Deleuze and Guattari argue, in a slightly different context, that it is a mistake to attach the image of interiority to Kafka's work. See Gilles Deleuze and Félix Guattari, *Kafka: Toward a Minor Literature* (Minneapolis: University of Minnesota Press, 1991), 45–46.

5. Much has been written about the incomplete and open-ended nature of Kafka's fiction. When his friend and literary executor Max Brod first prepared the manuscripts for publication after Kafka's death, he made significant editorial changes that rendered the novels "complete." Later editions adhere more strictly to the manuscripts themselves, and the restored translation of *The Castle*

by Mark Harmon (the edition used for this book) concludes with this unfinished sentence: "She held out her trembling hand to K. and had him sit down beside her, she spoke with great difficulty, it was difficult to understand her, but what she said" (It is the absence of punctuation that indicates the absence of an "ending.")

6. Raymond Roussel's prose offers a visible example of this architectonic mode—visible because the evidence is in the structure of the sentences rather than in their meaning. Roussel inserts multiple parenthetical phrases into his sentences. This geometry (the cleaving of the object [the sentence] to disrupt it by inserting a space, which is itself perhaps another object, then cleaved in order to insert another space, etc.) is a diagrammatic form that translates quite literally into real space. Roussel's sentences with their nested parentheses are perfectly architectural. A sentence that might acquire semantic momentum is forestalled and subverted by each successive parenthetical insertion. These create a fluid density, in which interruptions are the paradoxical device for establishing continuity. The middle becomes increasingly saturated, while the ends of the sentence (that is, the capital-letter beginning and the terminal punctuation) become increasingly remote from each other. Roussel's work is simultaneously opaque and transparent. Like nested Russian dolls, it is a relentless perpetuation of interiority. For example, the 1,276 alexandrines of *Nouvelles impressions d'Afrique* (written between 1915 and 1928 and published in 1932) are an exercise in a formally cultivated interiority that makes the subject of Africa nearly irrelevant.

7. Franz Kafka, *The Trial*, trans. Willa Muir and Edwin Muir (New York: Vintage Books, 1969), 15.

8. Ibid., 47.

9. Arthur Stanley Eddington, *The Nature of the Physical World* (New York: Cambridge University Press, 1929), 342; quoted in Walter Benjamin, "Some Reflections on Kafka," in *Illuminations*, ed.

Hannah Arendt, trans. Harry Zohn (New York: Schocken Books, 1969), 141.

10. Giorgio Agamben, *State of Exception*, trans. Kevin Attell (Chicago: University of Chicago Press, 2005), 59.

11. Michel Foucault writes of the cells of the Panopticon: "They are like so many theaters, in which each actor is alone, perfectly individualized and constantly visible." It is the very visibility that defines these prison interiors. At the Guantánamo prison, detainees are incarcerated in cages that place them deep within the interiority of surveillance, more exposed than even the Panoptic diagram. These cages are like those at the zoo; there is no escape from the spectator's gaze, or from the surveillance of the guards. It is the *gaze* that reinforces the enclosure and emphasizes interiority. The gaze captures and holds. Other prison stories demonstrate that opacity provides a certain freedom from this surveillance, which in turn opens possibilities for escape. Michel Foucault, *Discipline and Punish: The Birth of the Prison*, trans. Alan Sheridan (New York: Vintage Books, 1979), 201.

12. Like "Before the Law," "An Imperial Message" is separately published at the beginning of *Collected Stories*. Translators Edwin and Willa Muir called this section of the book "Two Introductory Parables," suggesting that together they provide an abstract introduction to the themes of Kafka's fiction.

13. See Borges's discussion of "Zeno's paradox against movement" as a precursor to Kafkan space: "Kafka and His Precursors," in *Labyrinths: Selected Stories and Other Writings*, ed. Donald A. Yates and James E. Irby (New York: Modern Library, 1983), 199.

14. This geometry describes an idealized diagram of the ancient imperial palace of Beijing.

Epigraph Horst Bienek, *The Cell* (London: Victor Gollancz, 1974), 25. Though *The Cell* is a novel, Bienek wrote from experience. While a pupil of Bertolt Brecht, he was arrested on political charges and sentenced to twenty-five years at the Vorkuta forced labor camp in Siberia. After four years he received amnesty, and went to live as a writer in West Germany. Of all the literature on imprisonment that I have read, this work is the most unforgiving, the most physical, and the most spatial.

15. While "deterritorialization" in Deleuze most often refers to the decodification of a system of signs within capital (i.e., liberating labor from its mode of production), here it refers to a displacement of power over the space of the cell. Bienek deterritorializes the cell through possessing the cell, a process of becoming not contained by it. That *becoming* is the blurring of the symbolic and real boundaries of self and cell.

16. If punishment ceases to be punishment, then the mechanism of the prison momentarily fails until it can *reterritorialize*—that is to say, until it can resignify the prisoner as prisoner and subsume this kind of reaction into its punitive design. "I own this cell; this cell is actually my room." Or "I am this cell, these walls, these objects." The prisoner creates conflict within the realm of symbolic order—the realm of signs—producing a new set of effects whereby he escapes and overcomes his role as prisoner. He uses his body not to suffer punishment but to resignify space; he establishes a line of flight. There is, of course, a glaring gap here: the prisoner remains a prisoner no matter his reaction. His line of flight has an enormous potential to fail because it remains within the realm of subjectivity and semiotics. It is a weak line of flight that undoubtedly curves back into the space of its origin. (In more overt escapes, boundaries to the interior are either directly violated or reinforced—any middle ground suggests an ordinary coping.) Bienek transforms not only cell into room but also himself from prisoner into free man. This is in marked contrast to the kind of escape that Deleuze and Guattari attribute to Kafka: "We would say that for Kafka, the animal essence is the way out, the

line of escape, even if it takes place in place, or in a cage." Deleuze and Guattari, *Kafka*, 35.

17. According to the architect Louis Kahn, "Architecture begins with the making of a room." These words are written on a charcoal drawing, c. 1972, at the Philadelphia Museum of Art.

18. Bertil Sandahl connects the Old French *rum, run*, meaning "ship's hold," and the Old Norse *rúm* "compartment of the hull," which he concludes lead to the English word "rummage," referring to the cargo stored in the ship's hold, between the thwarts. This is in the context of tracing the origins of the term "rom-nail," which he defines as "nails used when stowing wine-casks in the ship's hold ('room')." Further on, he speculates: "I think it is extremely likely that the use of **rum* and **rom*, doubtless in the wider sense 'ship's hold,' goes back to at least the 13th century." Bertil Sandahl, *Middle English Sea Terms*, vol. 1, *The Ship's Hull* (Uppsala: Lundequistska Bokhandeln, 1951), 153.

19. William Shakespeare, *Macbeth*, Act III, scene iv. Macbeth's aside:

> Then comes my fit again. I had else been perfect,
> Whole as the marble, founded as the rock,
> As broad and general as the casing air;
> But now I am cabin'd, cribb'd, confin'd, bound in
> To saucy doubts and fears—But Banquo's safe?

20. The Italian word for "room" is *stanza*. Closed forms of poetry, like the sonnet and the ballad, confine lines and rhymes within these formal "rooms." But the villanelle, a French form of six stanzas with overlapping rhymes and repetitions from stanza to stanza, is an open structure that allows entrances and exits at multiple points. Here is a representation of James Merrill's villanelle "The World and the Child," compared to Mies van der Rohe's Barcelona Pavilion. (These drawings first appeared in Stoner,

Poems for Architects [San Francisco: William Stout Publishers, 2001], 155.)

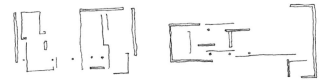

"The World and the Child"   *The Barcelona Pavilion*

21. Denis Hollier, *Against Architecture* (Cambridge: MIT Press, 1992), x.

22. John David Morley, *In the Labyrinth* (New York: Atlantic Monthly Press, 1986), 132–133.

23. Michael Faraday was commissioned by the Millbank Prison to conduct experiments on the auditory transmission capacity of various wall constructions. This is described and illustrated in Robin Evans, "The Rights of Retreat and the Rites of Exclusion: Notes toward a Definition of Wall," in *Translations from Drawings toward Building and Other Essays* (London: AA Journals, 2001), 41.

24. The Dirty War (*Guerra Sucia*) was a period of state-sponsored violence, torture, and execution in Argentina during the military dictatorship of Jorge Rafael Videla. It lasted from 1976 until 1983. Victims included trade unionists, students, journalists, Marxists, Peronist guerrillas, and their sympathizers, either proved or suspected. It is estimated that between 10,000 and 30,000 people were killed or disappeared.

25. Jacobo Timerman, *Prisoner without a Name, Cell without a Number*, trans. Toby Talbot (Madison: University of Wisconsin Press, 1981), 5.

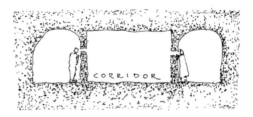

"An entire universe added to my Time."

26. Ibid., 6.

27. Gilles Deleuze and Félix Guattari, *A Thousand Plateaus: Capitalism and Schizophrenia*, trans. Brian Massumi (Minneapolis: University of Minnesota Press, 1987), 361.

Epigraph These are the famous lines in President Reagan's speech at the Brandenburg Gate on June 12, 1987, commemorating the 750th anniversary of the founding of Berlin. Reagan challenged Mikhail Gorbachev, then the general secretary of the Communist Party of the Soviet Union, to take down the Berlin Wall. Reagan was well aware of Gorbachev's desire to increase freedom in the Eastern bloc.

28. In the summer of 1989 I received a research grant to study the urban spatial condition of the Berlin Wall. With every expectation of finding the Wall intact, I planned the trip for early December. My son Ben and I we were thus among the first to be part of the Wall's physical destruction, purchasing one of the last available hammers at a hardware store in the Kreuzberg district. I was able to return to Berlin again in the summer of 1990. At that point, the Wall was reduced to a few fragments of foundation, and the euphoria of two cities joined had given way to a

commercial fervor. Merchants of all ethnicities sold chunks of concrete that looked suspiciously neutral (though those with remnants of colorful graffiti fetched a higher price), and architects were already competing for opportunities to produce signature buildings to occupy the fallow swath of land that had once been called "the Death Zone."

29. Virilio's discussion of the phenomenon of anorthoscopic vision is in relation to Marcel Odenbach's video *Die Distanz zwischen mir und meinen Verlusten*, which is directly connected to the Berlin Wall condition: "An anorthoscopic *slit* for an anachronistic *wall*, an iron curtain that has just now disappeared, been wiped out, because the people involved no longer believed in the totalitarian ideology imposed upon them for too long." Paul Virilio, "A Glimpse," in *A Landscape of Events*, trans. Julie Rose (Cambridge: MIT Press, 2000), 38–42.

30. In an essay written in the summer of 1987, Peter Schneider quotes a West German minister as having said, "Sometimes I think that the wall is the only thing holding the two Germanys together." Peter Schneider, "When the Wall Came Tumbling Down," *New York Times*, June 25, 1987.

31. In 1945 the Potsdam agreement established four zones of Allied occupation in Germany, and Berlin was similarly subdivided despite the city's location deep inside the Soviet zone.

32. Stealth, efficiency, and the incorporation of existing buildings into a politically motivated construction are all attributes of a minor architecture. It is the *politics from above* that places the Berlin Wall firmly in the realm of a majority construction.

33. Peter Schneider, *The Wall Jumper* (New York: Pantheon, 1983), 32.

34.   A mathematician named Klein
        Thought the Möbius band was divine
        Said he "If you glue

The edges of two,
You'll get a weird bottle like mine."
—Anonymous

In 1882 the German mathematician Felix Klein imagined sewing two Möbius strips together to create a single-sided bottle with no boundary. His idea was that its inside would be its outside; the bottle would contain itself. A true Klein bottle requires four dimensions, because the surface has to pass through itself without a hole. But relatively convincing drawings of its topology have been constructed, and actual bottles are now produced in glass. In these three-dimensional representations, the neck of the bottle (much like Benjamin's hand inside his sock) pulls itself through the interior to emerge out the other side. The Acme Klein Bottle Company sells zero-volume glass bottles in various configurations and sizes, and even a knitted "Klein Bottle Hat" (www. kleinbottle.com).

35. Walter Benjamin and Asja Lacis, "Naples," in Benjamin, *Reflections: Essays, Aphorisms, Autobiographical Writings*, ed. Peter Demetz, trans. Edmund Jephcott (New York: Harcourt Brace Jovanovich, 1978), 166–167.

36. In a similar spirit, John Berger writes of the paintings of Ralph Fassanella: "They present their interiors in such a way as to show they were never interiors. Nothing has an interior. Everything is exteriority." Fassanella accomplishes this by removing the facades from buildings; one sees in the paintings a set of domestic interiors exposed to the street, like porches in the air. John Berger, "Ralph Fassenella and the City," in *About Looking* (New York: Pantheon, 1980), 105.

Also in New York, E. B. White wrote of the neighborhoods of lower Manhattan in words that recall Benjamin's description of Naples: "All is cheerful and filthy and crowded. Small shops overflow onto the sidewalk, leaving only half the normal width for passers-by. In the candid light from unshaded bulbs gleam watermelon and lingerie. Families have fled the hot rooms upstairs and have found relief on the pavement. They sit on orange crates, smoking, relaxed, congenial. This is the nightly garden party of the vast Lower East Side—and on the whole they are more agreeable-looking hot-weather groups than some you see in bright canvas deck chairs on green lawns in country circumstances. . . . Overhead, like banners decorating a cotillion hall, stream the pants and bras from the pulley lines." E. B. White, *Here Is New York* (New York: Harper, 1949), 45.

Even today, in the old part of Naples known as Spacanapoli, such banners still fly high over the skinny streets (see photograph on page 37).

Epigraph John Updike, *Rabbit Redux* (New York: Alfred A. Knopf, 1971). This is the second of four novels in Updike's series about Harry Angstrom (whose nickname is Rabbit). In each, the time frame reflects the current time of Updike's own America. It is in this novel, taking place as the 1960s come to a close, that the physical, domestic environment most closely mirrors Rabbit's personal disillusionments.

37. The *American Heritage Dictionary* gives as the third definition of forest: "A defined area of land formerly set aside in England as a royal hunting ground."

38. Reconsidered according to their cumulative effect on the constructed landscape over more than a half-century, the interstate highways may be understood to have segmented the nation as much as smoothed it.

39. "He lived on Vista Crescent, third house from the end. Once there may have been here a vista, a softly sloped valley of red barns and fieldstone farmhouses, but more Penn Villas had been added and now the view from any window is as into a fragmented mirror, of houses like this." Updike, *Rabbit Redux*, 15.

40. Ibid., 25.

41. For a fictionalized account of the transformation of the quintessential American suburb, from its initial conceptualization in the late 1940s in the Levittowns of Pennsylvania and Long Island through to the next generation in the 1970s, see the story by W. D. Wetherell, "The Man Who Loved Levittown," in *The Man Who Loved Levittown* (New York: Avon Books, 1985), 1–17.

42. http://flightwise.com

43. See Indra Kagis McEwen, *Socrates' Ancestor* (Cambridge: MIT Press, 1994), 2.

44. Umberto Eco identifies this original Greek labyrinth as the first of three types: "If you unravel the classical labyrinth, you find a thread in your hand, the thread of Ariadne." The second type is the mannerist maze: "There is only one exit, but you can get it wrong." The third type is the rhizome: "The space of conjecture is a rhizome space." Umberto Eco, *Postscript to the Name of the Rose*, trans. William Weaver (San Diego: Harcourt Brace Jovanovich, 1984), 57.

45. For further discussion of *choros*, see McEwen, *Socrates' Ancestor*, 57–58, and Guy Davenport, "Ariadne's Dancing Floor," in *Every Force Evolves a Form* (San Francisco: North Point Press, 1987), 53–63.

46. This is Ovid's better-known version of the myth. In the story by Diodorus, Daedalus and Icarus escape by boat. In that version, Daedalus is credited with the invention not of wings but of sails. See McEwen, *Socrates' Ancestor*, 66–67.

47. For a discussion of the development of the nineteenth-century interior, see Charles Rice, *The Emergence of the Interior: Architecture, Modernity and Domesticity* (London: Routledge, 2007). For the twentieth-century development of the ideal of transparency, see the seminal essay by Colin Rowe and Robert Slutzky, "Transparency: Literal and Phenomenal," *Perspecta* 8 (1963); reprinted

in Colin Rowe, *The Mathematics of the Ideal Villa and Other Essays* (Cambridge: MIT Press, 1973).

48. In his essay "The Attic of the Brain," biologist Lewis Thomas draws a clever parallel between the rise of psychiatry as a practice and the disappearance of the attic from the American dwelling. For psychiatry, "the attic of the brain" is that storage space of the psyche not exposed to view. Thomas calls into question both the elimination of the attic and the "daylighting" of the subconscious, suggesting that a return of both the literal and the metaphorical attic might be a positive thing. Lewis Thomas, "The Attic of the Brain," in *Late Night Thoughts on Listening to Mahler's Ninth Symphony* (New York: Viking Press, 1983), 138–145.

49. Alain Robbe-Grillet, *For a New Novel* (New York: Grove Press, 1965).

50. Jeremy Bentham's Panopticon is only the most obvious of such diagrams of power.

51. The series was started in 1745. The first-state prints were published in 1750 and consisted of fourteen etchings, untitled and unnumbered. The original prints were 16 by 21 inches. For the second publishing in 1761 all the etchings were reworked and numbered I–XVI. Numbers II and V were new etchings to the series. Numbers I through IX were all done in portrait format (taller than they are wide), while X to XVI were landscape (wider than they are tall). Piranesi's *Carceri* etchings have now acquired generally agreed-upon working titles that allude to the spatial and architectural elements. For an account of the vertiginous and infinite quality of these drawings, see Thomas De Quincey's account of the description given him by Samuel Taylor Coleridge, in *Confessions of an English Opium-Eater* (1821).

III THE MYTH OF THE OBJECT

Epigraph Benjamin speaks with the love and passion of the collector; his
affection for his books has nothing to do with their resale value.
This short meditation was written while unpacking his library
(the boxes had been in storage for two years), and ends with a particularly "architectural" moment: "So I have erected one of his
dwellings, with books as the building stones, before you, and now
he is going to disappear inside, as is only fitting." Walter Benjamin, "Unpacking My Library," in *Illuminations*, ed. Hannah
Arendt, trans. Harry Zohn (New York: Schocken Books, 1969), 67.

1. Politics and the formation of blocks come together in American
   urban redevelopment strategies of the 1960s and '70s. City agen-
   cies authorized the agglomeration of smaller parcels, often including residential and small commercial use, into much larger
   blocks. This entailed the erasure of smaller streets and alleys and
   allowed the development of full-block corporate towers. In San
   Francisco, the transformation of what is now known as the Finan-
   cial District through these agglomeration strategies is particularly
   striking.

2. My thoughts on the concept of an architectural field were first
   developed in "The Jar and the Field," in *The Architecture of the In-
   Between*, Proceedings of the 78th Annual Meeting of the Associ-
   ation of Collegiate Schools of Architecture (Washington, DC:
   ACSA, 1990). "The Jar and the Field" is also the title of the
   fourth section of my book *Poems for Architects* (San Francisco:
   William Stout Publishers, 2001), in which I trace a spatial gene-
   alogy from architectural object to contingent field through a
   series of twentieth-century poems, beginning with Wallace Stevens's "Anecdote of the Jar" and ending with Mark Strand's
   "Keeping Things Whole."

3. John Berger writes of a field's contingency: "Suddenly a period of
   disinterested observation opens at its center and gives birth to a

happiness that is entirely your own. The field you are standing before seems to have the same dimensions as your own life." Berger, "Field," in *About Looking* (New York: Pantheon, 1980), 197–198.

4. Henri Lefebvre wrote: "The fact is that around 1910 a certain space was shattered. It was the space of common sense, of knowledge, of social practice, of political power . . . ; the space too of classical perspective and geometry." Lefebvre, *The Production of Space*, trans. Donald Nicholson-Smith (Oxford: Blackwell, 1991), 25. Virginia Woolf also cites 1910 as a watershed year, in her famous essay "Mr Bennet and Mrs Brown": "On or about December 1910, human character changed." Woolf, *The Collected Essays* (London: Hogarth Press, 1966), 320.

5. Cubist painters challenged the privileged status of the object relative to the air surrounding it; the canvas-as-field became the integrated composition of *all* elements within the painting. As Georges Braque described his method, "The space between the pitcher and the plate, I paint that also." See Thomas Vargish and Delo E. Mook, *Inside Modernism: Relativity Theory, Cubism, Narrative* (New Haven: Yale University Press, 1999).

Epigraph This passage is from "Burnt Norton," the first section of the "Four Quartets." T. S. Eliot, "Four Quartets," in *The Complete Poems and Plays* (London: Faber and Faber, 2004), 175.

6. Jennifer Bloomer correctly argues that a vessel's most important attribute is its function as container and conduit, as both "the sea and the ship." (The first of these functions is not acknowledged in the poems by Keats, Stevens, and Eliot.) See Jennifer Bloomer, *Architecture and the Text: The (S)crypts of Joyce and Piranesi* (New Haven: Yale University Press, 1993), 95, 184–192.

7. John Keats, "Ode on a Grecian Urn," the final two lines, attributed to the voice of the urn: "Beauty is truth, truth beauty, — that is all / Ye know on earth, and all ye need to know."

8. See "On Stuttering," in Constantin V. Boundas and Dorothea Olkowski, eds., *Gilles Deleuze and the Theater of Philosophy* (London: Routledge, 1996).

9. The most universal language of lazarine communication is known as "the quadratic alphabet":

A	B	C	D	E
F	G	H	I	J
L	M	N	O	P
Q	R	S	T	U
V	W	X	Y	Z

Like Morse code, each letter of the alphabet is defined by a precise sequence of taps. "Quadratic" refers to the organization of the code into a square grid of twenty-five letters. (In English, the letter K is omitted.) The code is explained fully in Arthur Koestler's novel *Darkness at Noon*. On the first day of his incarceration, the central character Rubashov (familiar with the code from previous times in prison) easily deciphers the first message from his neighbor in cell no. 402: "WHO?" Arthur Koestler, *Darkness at Noon* (New York: Macmillan, 1941), 25–28.

10. Franz Kafka, *The Castle*, trans. Mark Harmon (New York: Schocken Books, 1998), 71–72.

11. According to Max Brod, Kafka based this village on the town of Zurau in the Urz Mountains. Cited in Walter Benjamin, "Franz Kafka," in *Illuminations*, ed. Hannah Arendt, trans. Harry Zohn (New York: Schocken Books, 1969).

12. Deleuze and Guattari offer an analysis of two distinct architectural states in Kafka's novels. The first state is vertical—the allegorical Castle as a literally hierarchical form. The second state is horizontal, yet escapes true perspective. What is most striking in their analysis is the paradoxical linking of discontinuity with nearness (for example, the relationship of the Castle to the rooms at the Inn) and contiguity with distance (the door from Titorelli's room that leads to the court). Staircases and towers reinforce the model of the former state, low ceilings and long corridors the latter. Gilles Deleuze and Félix Guattari, *Kafka: Toward a Minor Literature* (Minneapolis: University of Minnesota Press, 1991), 74–78.

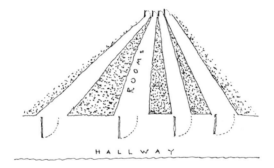

Continuous and discontinuous doorways at the Gentleman's Inn.
—after Deleuze and Guatarri

13. Following Agamben, we can also argue that the castle is in the shadow of the camp: "The camp, which is now securely lodged within the city's interior, is the new biopolitical *nomos* of the planet." Here the Camp becomes the new law; all other space is within its rule. Giorgio Agamben, *Homo Sacer: Sovereign Power and Bare Life*, trans. Daniel Heller-Roazen (Stanford: Stanford University Press, 1998), 176.

14. Elias Canetti's *Crowds and Power* develops a unique anthropological approach to the comprehension of crowds and their structure. Like Arendt, he defines the crowd as a single unit that renders impotent the small units within. But he locates the precedent for the crowd image differently for every culture, in each case identifying a natural feature as the model. For the Mongols, it is the molecules of air that make up the wind; for the Arabs, the grains of sand in the desert. For the Germans, it is the forest within which the upright trees become indistinguishable one from the other. Canetti, *Crowds and Power*, trans. Carol Stewart (Harmondsworth: Penguin, 1973).

15. Foucault describes distinct mechanisms of exclusion for plague and leprosy. For plague: "First, a strict partitioning: the closing of the town and its outlying districts, a prohibition to leave the town on pain of death, the killing of all stray animals; the division of the town into distinct quarters, each governed by an intendant. . . . It is a segmented, immobile, frozen space." Michel Foucault, *Discipline and Punish* (New York: Vintage Books, 1979), 195.

16. Even in the wake of the Holocaust, and as part of its memorialization, the massing of objects in various museum exhibits (eyeglasses, shoes) continues the sublimation of multiplicity (an assemblage of individuals) through an objectified "block" (a singularity chosen for its effect).

17. "Jewish Residential Quarter" and "relocation to the east" were the euphemistic names given by the Reich to the Warsaw Ghetto and the deportations to the death camps.

18. "Now, in December 1942, hiding places are very popular. Everyone is making them. Everywhere, in all the shops and elsewhere in the Ghetto, hiding places are being built. Their construction has actually become a flourishing specialized craft. Skilled workers, engineers, etc. are making a living out of it. Hiding places go back many years. . . . On Franciszkanska and Nalewki Streets,

cellars were walled up, attics, special rooms, stores of merchandise." Emmanuel Ringelblum, *Notes from the Warsaw Ghetto: Journal of Emmanuel Ringelblum*, trans. and ed. Jacob Sloane (New York: Schocken Books, 1974), 338.

19. Israel Gutman, *Resistance: The Warsaw Ghetto Uprising* (New York: Houghton Mifflin, 1994), 196. The drawing on the left (below) represents a simplified street plan of the fourth and final state of the ghetto in 1943. On the right is a conjectural plan of the underground labyrinth of bunkers and tunnels.

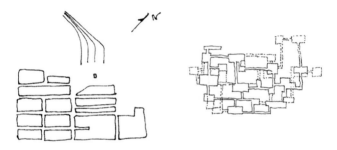

20. In another part of Warsaw, a group of Polish partisans employed similar underground tactics. I first became aware of these subterranean, labyrinthine spaces of resistance through my friend and former colleague Władysław Strumiłło, who fought in the Warsaw uprising of 1944. (The uprising in the Jewish ghetto took place one year earlier.) Strumiłło's paper on the subject, written in 1980 but never published, is titled "Environmental Means of Control and Resistance: Case Study Warsaw."

21. The eventual destruction of the ghetto was by fire and chemicals, rather than through spatial means.

22. Deleuze and Guattari, *Kafka*, 17.

23. Walter Benjamin distinguishes "mythic violence" from "divine violence," as violence associated respectively with institutions of

law and purely political acts. He concludes: "Pure divine violence is free . . . to adopt any of the everlasting forms that myth has bastardized with law." Benjamin, "Critique of Violence," trans. Edmund Jephcott, in *One Way Street and Other Writings* (London: NLB, 1979), 28.

Giorgio Agamben draws upon this distinction in developing his theory of a "state of exception." He writes: "Politics has suffered a lasting eclipse because it has been contaminated by law, seeing itself, at best, as a constituent power (that is, violence that makes law), when it is not reduced to merely the power to negotiate with the law. The only truly political action, however, is that which severs the nexus between violence and law." Giorgio Agamben, *State of Exception*, trans. Kevin Attell (Chicago: University of Chicago Press, 2005), 88.

24. Agamben, building upon a theory first developed by Carl Schmitt in 1922, defines the "state of exception" thus: "The exception is what cannot be included in the whole of which it is a member and cannot be a member of the whole in which it is always already included." Agamben, *Homo Sacer*, 25. Agamben wrote *State of Exception* in 2003 as a sequel to *Homo Sacer*. In the more recent book, his argument incorporates certain political developments in the United States— specifically the repercussions of the Patriot Act—following the aftermath of September 11, 2001.

25. This definition of "space of exception" has equal allegiance to the etymological origins of "exception"—from *exceptus*, "taken out." These spaces of exception are literally the escape, or the "flight," from the object/subject.

26. Agamben develops the concept of *bare life* around the subject of the camp inmate, the prisoner who is neither citizen nor slave but part of a surplus, excluded, and liminal population. In his introduction to *Homo Sacer*, he begins by explaining the important distinction between two Greek words for life. *Bios* is life with purpose, the kind of life made possible by politics. *Zoe* is the life

common to animals, humans, and gods; it is nothing *but* life (thus, "bare life"). Agamben, *Homo Sacer*, 1–12.

27. Margaret Atwood's dystopian novel *The Handmaid's Tale* (New York: Anchor Books, 1986), perhaps more than any other work of fiction, brings these two worlds together. In a fascist patriarchy that calls itself the Republic of Gilead, all women are assigned to various roles of subjugation. The setting is described as an ordinary American suburb of the 1980s. It is the juxtaposition of these two conditions that gives the novel much of its power.

A more satiric and explicit image of the same juxtaposition is found in J. G. Ballard's novel *Super Cannes*: "Strains of suburban fascism. . . . Surveillance cameras hung like gargoyles from the cornices, following me as I approached the barbican and identified myself to the guard at the reception desk. . . . High above me, fluted columns carried the pitched roofs, an attempt at a vernacular architecture that failed to disguise this executive-class prison. Taking their cue from Eden-Olympia and Antibes-les-Pins, the totalitarian systems of the future would be subservient and ingratiating, but the locks would be just as strong." J. G. Ballard, *Super Cannes* (London: Picador, 2002).

28. As early as 1949, Leo Lowenthal perceived a similarity between these two kinds of regime. As a Jew and a member of the Frankfurt School, Lowenthal had fled Germany in 1933 when Hitler came to power. During World War II, he worked in Washington for the Office of War Information. It was here, in the years immediately after the war, that he began to perceive first the undercurrents and then the more explicit political agendas that culminated in the McCarthy witch hunts. In his autobiography he reflects: "Today I sometimes have to laugh at my naïveté then. I didn't realize the internal mobility and politicization of the governmental apparatus. I finally came into great difficulties when the Republicans took over the helm and, besides that, the entire agency was transferred to the organizational

framework of the U.S. Information Agency. Then they made my life very tough, broke up my department, and reduced my research funding in order gradually to force me to quit." Leo Lowenthal, *An Unmastered Past*, ed. Martin Jay (Berkeley: University of California Press, 1987), 86.

29. This is at least partly the result of the emigration of architects like Mies van der Rohe and Walter Gropius to the United States. The social missions of the European modernists, as developed through the CIAM conferences of the 1930s, were replaced with more formal agendas that served the interests of free market capitalism.

30. See Paul Groth, "Lot, Yard, and Garden: American Gardens as Adorned Yards," *Landscape* 30, no. 3(1990), 29–35.

31. Lefebvre has this to say about the commodity paradox: "What is a commodity? A concrete abstraction. An abstraction certainly— but not an abstraction *in spite of* its status as a thing; an abstraction, on the contrary, *on account of* its status as a social 'thing,' divorced, during its existence, from its materiality, from the use to which it is put, from productive activity, and from the need that it satisfies. And concrete, just as certainly, by virtue of its practical power. The commodity is a social 'being-there,' an 'object' irreducible to the philosophical concept of the Object. The commodity hides in stores, in warehouses—in inventory. Yet it has no mystery comparable to the mystery of nature. The enigma of the commodity is entirely social. It is the enigma of money and property, of specific needs and the demand-money-satisfaction cycle. The commodity asks for nothing better than to *appear*. And appear it does—visible/readable, in shop windows and on display racks. Self-exhibition is its forte. Once it is apparent, there is no call to decode it; it has no need of decipherment after the fashion of the 'beings' of nature and of the imagination. And yet, once it has appeared, its mystery only deepens.

Who has produced it? Who will buy it? Who will profit from its sale? Who, or what purpose, will it serve? Where will the money go? The commodity does not answer these questions; it is simply *there*, exposed to the gaze of passers-by, in a setting more or less alluring, more or less exhibitionistic, be it in a nondescript small shop or in a glittering department store." Lefebvre, *The Production of Space*, 341.

32. For a succinct and humorous comparison of the "useful" kind of dwelling embedded in the temporalities of daily life and its occasions with the overly commodified, frozen typology that replaced it in the 1960s and '70s, see Joan Didion's essay "Many Mansions." She compares the old governor's mansion in Sacramento (with its marble slab in the kitchen for rolling pie crusts, and easy chair in the bathroom for reading stories to a child in the bath) with the never-lived-in house built for Ronald and Nancy Reagan on the American River (with its kitchen for "defrosting by microwave and compacting trash"). Didion, "Many Mansions," in *The White Album* (New York: Washington Square Press, 1979), 67–78.

33. See J. G. Ballard's story "The Subliminal Man," in *The Complete Short Stories of J. G. Ballard* (New York: W. W. Norton, 2009), vol. 1.

34. We are here using Agamben's definition of an apparatus: "I will call an apparatus literally anything that has in some way the capacity to capture, determine, orient, intercept, model, control or secure the gestures, behaviors, opinions or discourses of living beings." Giorgio Agamben, "What Is an Apparatus?," in *What Is an Apparatus? and Other Essays*, trans. David Kishik and Stefan Pedatella (Stanford: Stanford University Press, 2009), 14.

35. John Cheever, "The Swimmer," in *Collected Stories and Other Writings* (New York: Library of America, 2009), 603–612.

Cheever originally intended this to be a novel based on the myth of Narcissus. The story is condensed from over 150 pages of notes.

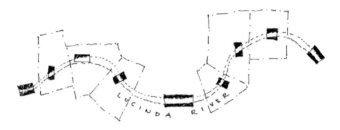

"He seemed to see, with a cartographer's eye, that string of swimming pools. . . ."

Epigraph Nietzsche goes on: "My thoughts," said the wanderer to his shadow, "should show me where I stand, but should not betray to me *where I am going*. I love ignorance of the future and do not want to perish of impatience and premature tasting of things promised." Friedrich Nietzsche, *The Gay Science*, ed. Bernard Williams (Cambridge: Cambridge University Press, 2001), 287.

36. I, Tiresias, though blind, throbbing between two lives,
Old man with wrinkled female breasts, *can see*
At the violet hour, the evening hour that strives
Homeward . . .

T. S. Eliot, "The Waste Land," lines 228–231, in *The Complete Poems and Plays*, 68 (emphasis mine), and notes on line 228, p. 78.

37. Ibid., 78.

38. www3.Wooster.edu/artfuldodge/interview/borges.

39. Borges traces the history of this idea back through time: "The library is a sphere whose exact center is any one of its hexagons and whose circumference is inaccessible" (Borges, twentieth century). "Nature is an infinite sphere whose center is everywhere,

whose circumference is nowhere" (Pascal, seventeenth century). "We can assert with certainty that the universe is all center, or that the center of the universe is everywhere, and its circumference is nowhere" (Giordano Bruno, sixteenth century). "God is an intelligible sphere whose center is everywhere and whose circumference is nowhere" (Alain de Lille, twelfth century). Jorge Luis Borges, "The Library of Babel" and "The Fearful Sphere of Pascal," in *Labyrinths: Selected Stories and Other Writings*, ed. Donald A. Yates and James E. Irby (New York: Modern Library, 1983), 51–58, 189–192.

40. Asked once to comment on the poems of Federico García Lorca, Borges said: "But I'm not fond of Lorca. Well you see, this is a shortcoming of mine, I dislike visual poetry. He is visual all the time, and he goes in for fancy metaphors." See www3.Wooster.edu/artfuldodge/interview/borges.

41. As Guy Davenport writes, "The imagination is like the drunk man who loses his watch, and must get drunk again to find it." Davenport, *The Geography of the Imagination* (San Francico: North Point Press, 1983), 5.

42. Raymond Carver, "Cathedral," in *Cathedral* (New York: Vintage Press, 1983), 218.

43. Ibid., 225.

44. Ibid., 228.

45. "Je dis: une fleur! Et, hors de l'oubli où ma voix relègue aucun contour, en tant que quelque chose d'autre que les calices sus, musicalement se lève, idée même et suave, l'absente de tous bouquets." Stéphane Mallarmé, "Crise de vers," in *Oeuvres complètes* (Paris: Gallimard, 1945), 368.

Epigraph Paul Klee, *On Modern Art* (London: Faber and Faber, 1949), 53. There is one drawing in particular that fits this description exactly, on page 50.

46. Paul Valéry, *Introduction to the Method of Leonardo da Vinci*, trans. Thomas McGreevy (London: John Rodker, 1929), 17.

47. Now what used to be drafting (the name no longer applies) is a different kind of process—tapping keys and clicking mice substitute for pulling lead. The lines of a computer-generated drawing are not lines of force, though some softwares use scripts to generate lines in a repeating sequence. Most often these methods are used to make form. Perhaps we have not yet fully comprehended their capacity to clear space.

48. Paul Klee, *Pedagogical Sketchbooks* (New York: Nierendorf Gallery, 1944), I.1. "An active line which moves freely, a walk for a walk's sake, without aim. The agent is a shifting point."

49. Paul Valéry, quoted in Italo Calvino, *Six Memos for the Next Millennium* (New York: Vintage Books, 1988), 16. This is one of Calvino's references to the virtue of lightness in literature. A bird is light with a force; it literally represents a line of flight. We might infer (for our purposes) that a feather is light only in weight. It is without agency, direction, or desire.

50. "Language stops being representative in order to now move toward its extremities or its limits." Deleuze and Guattari, *Kafka*, 23.

51. In the winter of 1989, on an overnight train from Berlin to Warsaw, I played a game of chess with a young Polish man from Poznán. Though he was extremely tired and fell asleep after nearly every move, he won the game. He explained to me that he approached each move as a reaction to an unstable field; his strategy was not temporal (like a military operation) but spatial. The root of the name Poland, *pol*, means field, and I later reflected that this man's description of a game played as a reaction to

immediate spatial qualities described well his country's bare survival through the events of the twentieth century. See Jill Stoner, "Camp and Field: Notes on the Polish Landscape," *Traditional Dwellings and Settlements Review* 3, no. 1 (1991).

52. I refer here to games in the traditional sense—children's games, card games. (In the case of sports franchises, "game" is a word attached to a commodified enterprise. Both the players and their field are converted to apparatuses that support an agenda driven by capital.)

IV   THE MYTH OF THE SUBJECT

1. "And they said, Go to, let us build us a city and a tower, whose top may reach unto heaven; and let us make us a name, lest we be scattered abroad upon the face of the whole earth." Genesis 11:1–9.

2. Originally called the Burj Dubai, the building was renamed Burj Khalifa in honor of the mayor of Dubai, who helped finance its completion. As of this writing, the tower is only 10 percent occupied.

3. Paul Valéry, "Eupalinos, or the Architect," in *Dialogues*, trans. William McCausland Stewart, *Collected Works of Paul Valéry*, vol. 4 (New York: Pantheon Books, 1956), 81. It is important to note that Valéry meant something different when he wrote these lines—not that the constructions give identity to the constructor, but that the self is discovered through the *act* of construction: "I seem to myself to have made of the existence that was given me a sort of human handiwork." The dialogue is discussed at greater length in chapter V.

4. Beatriz Colomina has a different interpretation of space and the production of the subject: "Architecture is not simply a platform that accommodates the viewing subject. It is a viewing mechanism

that produces the subject." Colomina, "The Split Wall: Domestic Voyeurism," in Colomina, ed., *Sexuality and Space* (New York: Princeton Architectural Press, 1992), 83.

5. In March of 1974, Kahn died unrecognized in a men's room at New York's Penn Station, his office deeply in debt. For some reason he had crossed out the address on his passport, and he lay in the morgue for several days before being identified. Today, it is difficult to imagine an architect of his stature traveling without an entourage.

6. It is important to distinguish Kahn's concept of the "institution" from that of Foucault. Kahn's "institutions" are the very substance of democracy, the essence of the building's intended use. He gave to institutions three shared inspirations: the inspiration to learn, the inspiration to meet, and the inspiration for well-being.

   Foucault, on the other hand, used the concept of the institution to describe mechanisms of exclusion, segregation, and control, as in the asylum, the hospital, the military academy, and the prison. It is from this semantic interpretation that we speak of "institutionalizing" certain populations, thereby casting them simultaneously *in* to a hermetic interior and *out* to the margins.

7. J. G. Ballard, *High Rise* (London: Jonathan Cape, 1975), 9.

8. Ibid., 1.

9. Hannah Arendt frames the human condition through the successive states of labor, work, and action. Arendt, *The Human Condition* (New York: Doubleday, 1959), sections III, IV, V.

10. For an in-depth discussion of the emergence of the concept of the user, see the essay titled "User" in Adrian Forty, *Words and Buildings: A Vocabulary of Modern Architecture* (London: Thames and Hudson, 2000).

11. The place of consumption (the mall, for example) confirms the subject's identity precisely through the objects consumed. The place of the subject is at the intersection of these objects; it becomes the locus of a specious, illusory comfort. Minor architectures erase the coordinates that define a subject's position in relation to commodities.

12. In his book on Foucault, Deleuze describes *The Archaeology of Knowledge* as "the most decisive step yet taken in the theory-practice of multiplicities." Gilles Deleuze, *Foucault*, trans. Seán Hand (Minneapolis: University of Minnesota Press, 1988), 14.

Epigraph This is my own translation. The original French text reads, "Donner un sens plus pur aux mots de la tribu." C. F. MacIntyre's translation is "with a sense more pure the words of the tribe," and Mallarmé himself made an English translation for Sarah Helen Whitman (to whom Poe once proposed marriage): "To give too pure a meaning to the words of the tribe." Stéphane Mallarmé, *Poems*, trans. C. F. MacIntyre (Berkeley: University of California Press, 1971), 88, 89, 151.

13. Gilles Deleuze and Félix Guattari, *A Thousand Plateaus: Capitalism and Schizophrenia*, trans. Brian Massumi (Minneapolis: University of Minnesota Press, 1987), 3.

14. Roland Barthes, "Death of the Author," trans. Richard Howard, in *Image, Music, Text* (New York: Hill and Wang, 1977), 146.

15. These lines from Neruda were translated by Alistair Reid and hung as a banner at City Lights Books in San Francisco, June 2003. My thanks to Jim Dennon for the reference.

16. In fiction also, Poe deemphasizes character and gives character to space. His architectural settings are the original spatial protagonists of literature: the House of Usher, subterranean wine cellars, a torture chamber of the Spanish Inquisition. Scarcely recognized in the United States during his lifetime, Poe nevertheless had an

enormous influence abroad, particularly in France among the symbolist poets.

17. Deleuze unpacks Leibniz's house in his study of the baroque: *The Fold* (trans. Tom Conley; Minneapolis: University of Minnesota Press, 1993). The first chapter is devoted to the bottom floor: "the pleats of matter"; the second chapter is the floor above: "the folds of the soul."

18. "Il quitte la chamber et se perd dans les escaliers" ("He leaves the room and loses himself in the stairs"; my translation). Stéphane Mallarmé, *Igitur* (Paris: Gallimard, 1925), 43.

19. This image of a dice throw became the subject of Mallarmé's long poem *Un coup de dés jamais n'abolira le hasard* (A throw of the dice will never abolish chance).

20. J. G. Ballard, *Concrete Island* (New York: Vintage, 1985), 11.

21. Ibid., 71.

22. "Even their present house had been designed to avoid the hazards of over-familiarity." Ibid., 76.

23. *Imagining Argentina* is the first in a trilogy about the *desaparecidos* of Buenos Aires in the 1970s. Lawrence Thornton, *Imagining Argentina* (New York: Doubleday, 1987).

24. Of those missing persons taken by force during the Dirty War, Argentine de facto president General Jorge Rafael Videla said in a press conference: "They are neither dead nor alive, they are *desaparecidos*." International human rights law has since introduced the legal term "forced disappearances."

25. Thornton, *Imagining Argentina*, 179.

26. Julia Kristeva describes a text that "exists only if it can find a reader who matches its rhythms." Kristeva, *Desire in Language*, quoted in Jennifer Bloomer, *Architecture and the Text: The (S)crypts of Joyce and Piranesi* (New Haven: Yale University Press, 1993), 163.

27. Thornton, *Imagining Argentina*, 182.

"They have taken Teresa away."

28. Even the hardest materials become "soft" with repetitive and collective use over time. We can see this in the worn steps of Wells Cathedral, or the rubbed turnstiles of the New York subway. Saul Bellow writes: "Innumerable millions of passengers had polished the wood of the turnstile with their hips. From this arose a feeling of communion—brotherhood in one of its cheapest forms." Saul Bellow, *Herzog* (New York: Viking Press, 1964), 176.

29. With regard to Cecelia's mnemonic system, see Ellen Eve Frank, *Literary Architecture: Essays toward a Tradition; Walter Pater, Gerard Manley Hopkins, Marcel Proust, Henry James* (Berkeley: University of California Press, 1979), 280.

30. Le Corbusier made clear his belief in the importance of authorial intentions when he wrote of the schist heaps in Flanders: "Those are not masterpieces; those are not works of art. Here there is nothing more than an industrial enterprise in which no elevated

intention is involved." Le Corbusier, *When the Cathedrals Were White: A Journey to the Country of Timid People*, trans. Francis Hyslop (London: Routledge, 1947), 25.

31. Yamasaki was also the architect of the World Trade Center towers in Manhattan, begun in 1966, completed in 1973, and destroyed in terrorist attacks on September 11, 2001.

32. Jencks continues: "Pruitt-Igoe was constructed according to the most progressive ideals of CIAM . . . and it had won an award from the American Institute of Architects when it was designed in 1951. It consisted of elegant slab blocks fourteen storeys high with rational 'streets in the air' (which were safe from cars, but as it turned out, not safe from crime); 'sun, space, and greenery,' which Corbusier had called the 'three essential joys of urbanism' (instead of conventional streets, gardens, and semi-private space, which he banished). It had a separation of pedestrian and vehicular traffic, the provision of play space, and local amenities such as laundries, crèches, and gossip centres—all rational substitutes for traditional patterns. Moreover, its purist style, its clean, salubrious hospital metaphor, was meant to instill, by good example, corresponding virtues in the inhabitants. Good form was to lead to good content, or at least good conduct; the intelligent planning of abstract space was to promote healthy behaviour." Charles Jencks, *The Language of Post-Modern Architecture*, 5th ed. (London: Academy Editions, 1987), 9.

33. In spring 2008 I brought a group of Berkeley students to Rome to study Corviale and make design proposals for its future. The drawing below, based on a scheme by Ashley Thomas, suggests threads of light woven vertically into the concrete fabric.

Immediately after the Italian elections in spring 2010, incoming Lazio regional councilor Teodoro Buontempo announced that he plans to tear Corviale down. The intention is to replace "the Giant Serpent" with a high-density mixed-use development. It remains to be seen how this new proposal will play out. As of this writing, the website http://www.planetizen.com/node/44338 features the debate on the proposed demolition, and illustrations of three "new urbanist" alternatives designed by Italian architects.

34. Francesco Careri, *Walkscapes: Walking as an Aesthetic Practice* (Barcelona: Gustavo Gili, 2003).

35. Careri writes: "Stalker is a collective of architects and researchers connected to the *Roma Tre* University who came together in the mid-1990s. In 2002, Stalker founded the research network *Osservatorio Nomade (ON)*, which consists of architects, artists, activists and researchers working experimentally and engaging in actions to create self-organised spaces and situations. Stalker have developed a specific methodology of urban research, using participative tools to construct a 'collective imaginary' for a place. In particular they have developed the method of collective walking to 'actuate territories,' which for them is a process of bringing space into being. Stalker carry out their walks in the 'indeterminate' or void spaces of the city, which have long been disregarded or considered a problem in traditional architectural practice. Since their early walks, Stalker/ON have developed an approach to architecture that is profoundly participatory. Using tactical and playful interventions, they aim at creating spatial transformations through engaging in social relations, because as they have observed, the built environment takes too long to respond to the needs and desires of those who inhabit it." (www.stalkeron.it) The Corviale project is published in "ON—Osservatorio Nomade—Stalker: Immaginare Corviale, Rome, Italy 2004–2005," *A + U: Architecture and Urbanism* (2005).

36. http://talkingcities.org/talkingcities/pages/180_en.html.

37. Albert Camus referred to Kafka's characters as "automata": "And those 'inspired automata' provide us with a precise image of what we should be if we were deprived of our distractions, and utterly consigned to the humiliations of the divine." Camus, "Hope and the Absurd in the Work of Franz Kafka," in *The Myth of Sisyphus and Other Essays* (New York: Alfred A. Knopf, 1955), 131.

38. Benjamin's discussion of the "Oklahoma Nature Theater" chapter of *Amerika* emphasizes the importance of the gesture in Kafka's work. Walter Benjamin, "Franz Kafka," in *Illuminations*, 119–122.

39. In one section of the Trial, K. opens the door of his office at the bank leading to an adjacent room and discovers that the warders initially present at his arrest are being whipped. The next day the scene is exactly the same. Time has seemed to pass, but in the world of the warders (and his own world) nothing has happened. This is a temporal paradox congruent with the spatial one that inexplicably moves the Court from the other end of town to Titorelli's building.

40. Walter Benjamin, "Some Reflections on Kafka," in *Illuminations*, ed. Hannah Arendt, trans. Harry Zohn (New York: Schocken Books, 1969), 144.

41. Gilles Deleuze and Félix Guattari, *Kafka: Toward a Minor Literature* (Minneapolis: University of Minnesota Press, 1991), 42.

42. "To do justice to the figure of Kafka in its purity and its peculiar beauty one must never lose sight of one thing: it is the purity and beauty of failure." Benjamin, "Some Reflections on Kafka," 144–145.

43. Walter Benjamin, "The Destructive Character," in *Reflections: Essays, Aphorisms, Autobiographical Writings*, ed. Peter Demetz, trans. Edmund Jephcott (New York: Harcourt Brace Jovanovich, 1978), 542.

V THE MYTH OF NATURE

Epigraph *De rerum natura* (usually translated into English as *On the Nature of Things*) is a first-century BC epic poem by the Roman poet and philosopher Lucretius. His goal was to explain the principles of Epicurean philosophy to a Roman audience.

1. Dystopian fiction and films have continually reinforced the myth of nature as the "other." As early as 1921, Yevgeny Zamyatin's novel *We* was based in an antiseptic and highly ordered city, where numbered phalanxes of obedient workers are isolated from the primitive wilderness by a "green wall." We might call this "nature in exile." In the 1972 film *Silent Running*, directed by Douglas Trumbull, botanical systems on Earth have been so decimated by civilization that they exist only within two biospheres orbiting in the stratosphere, overseen by one mere mortal and two robot droids. This is "nature in protective custody."

2. Herman Melville, *Moby Dick* (London: J. M. Dent and Sons, 1977), 249.

Epigraph Valéry was commissioned to write the dialogue in 1927, as an introduction to a folio of plans and engravings. Paul Valéry, "Eupalinos, or the Architect," in *Dialogues*, vol. 4 of *The Collected Works of Paul Valéry* (New York: Pantheon, 1956), 145. I am forever in debt to bookstore owner Joseph Fox in Philadelphia, who first introduced me to Valéry's *Dialogues* in 1997. According to Fox, it was a favorite text of Louis Kahn. Wallace Stevens, the poet Kahn referred to most often, wrote an introduction to the Pantheon edition of the *Dialogues* shortly before his death.

3. We know this because Phaedrus refers to Mallarmé ("the very admirable Stephanos, who appeared so many centuries after us"), who died in 1898. Valéry, "Eupalinos," 67.

4. It turned out that Valéry chose the name Eupalinos almost at random. He learned later that Eupalinos was more an engineer than

an architect, better known for digging canals than constructing temples.

5. In expressing his inclination toward architecture, Socrates indirectly returns us to the ur-architect Daedalus, who (according to Plato's *Euthyphro*) is Socrates' ancestor. See Indra Kagis McEwen, *Socrates' Ancestor* (Cambridge: MIT Press, 1994), 1–2. Valéry, while not claiming any Greek or mythic ancestry, was also drawn to architecture, as is first expressed in *Introduction to the Method of Leonardo da Vinci* (1895) and also in the play *Amphion* (1931).

6. Valéry, "Eupalinos," 145ff.

7. Gilles Deleuze and Félix Guattari, *Kafka: Toward a Minor Literature* (Minneapolis: University of Minnesota Press, 1991), 23.

8. I first wrote about the peregrine falcon's reterritorialization in the essay "The Falcon's Return," *Places* 12, no. 3 (1999). See also Lisa Couturier, "Heirloom," in *The Hope of Snakes* (Boston: Beacon Press, 2005), 36–45.

9. http://www2.edu//nestcameras.htm.

10. Deleuze and Guattari give as specific examples of deterritorialization and reterritorialization the development of the human hand on the northern steppes (a deterritorialization) and the subsequent adaptation of the foot (a reterritorialization), also on the steppes. Gilles Deleuze and Félix Guattari, *A Thousand Plateaus: Capitalism and Schizophrenia*, trans. Brian Massumi (Minneapolis: University of Minnesota Press, 1987), 68.

11. Anita Desai, "Pigeons at Daybreak," in Barbara H. Solomon, ed., *Other Voices, Other Vistas* (New York: Mentor, 1992).

12. Selected entries to the "Dead Malls" competition (including that of the author) are published in the *New York Times*, June 15, 2003; www.core77.com/reactor/deadmalls.asp; www.RetailTrafficMag.com/development/renovation/retail_visions_future; and "Visions of the Future," *Architecture*, April 2003.

13. See Nicholas de Monchaux, ed., *Network Infrastructures*, University of California, Berkeley, 2010.

14. Approximately the same number of people are currently living at Corviale.

15. Quoted in guardian.co.uk, July 20, 2011.

16. Ballard actually wrote, "I regret that no one could fall in love inside the Heathrow Hilton. By contrast, people are forever falling in love inside the Louvre and the National Gallery." This was in the context of articulating his admiration for architectural modernism, and referenced in particular the Heathrow Hilton in London. J. G. Ballard, "A Handful of Dust," *Guardian*, March 20, 2006.

17. Valéry, "Eupalinos," 148.

18. Valéry wrote "Eupalinos" in 1927; though modernism was gradually taking hold in Europe, the Ecole des Beaux-Arts still held sway in architectural education. His reflections on architecture are completely consistent with the long Western tradition that revered a classical notion of beauty, one generated through visual canons of proportion, materiality, and detail. I am simply speculating freely on how Valéry's synthetic mind might have absorbed the political and ecological developments of the late twentieth century, and how his thoughts about architecture might have developed as a result.

19. Here I am paraphrasing Annie Dillard: "A book no one is reading is like Victoria Falls, or a zoo at night, its internal activities unperceived. . . . The bright lights of a book no one is reading bounce around inside its binding unseen." Dillard, *Living by Fiction* (New York: Harper Colophon, 1982), 175.

page viii   Church ruins, Detroit, 1991

page xii   *Twelve Monkeys*, directed by Terry Gilliam, 1992

page 17   San Francisco Airport Hilton, photograph by Ibone Santiago, 2011

page 20   *The Trial*, directed by Orson Wells, 1961

page 25   *The Trial*, directed by Orson Wells, 1961

page 34   Berlin Wall, photographer unknown, 1961

page 37   Spacanapoli, 2006

page 44   "EXIT," photograph by Hope Mitnick, 1995

page 46   *The Swimmer*, directed by Frank Perry, 1968

page 70   *Fahrenheit 451*, directed by François Truffaut, 1966

page 83   *Imagining Argentina*, directed by Christopher Hampton, 2003

page 87   Corviale, 2008

page 90   East Oakland School of the Arts, Stoner Meek Architecture and
             Urban Design, 2006

page 92   *Twelve Monkeys*, directed by Terry Gilliam, 1992

page 98   George and Gracie, 2008

page 101   Michigan Theater, Detroit, 1991

page 106   "AVAILABLE," photograph by Ibone Santiago, 2011

page 108   Jewish cemetery in Prague, photograph by Ben Stoner-Duncan, 1990

All photographs, unless otherwise noted, are by the author. The drawings on
pages 67, 78, 123, 124, 133, 135, 140, 147, and 148 are by the author.

All reasonable efforts have been made to trace the source of the photograph
on page 34. Any relevant information brought to the author's attention will
be acknowledged in later printings.

FICTION AND POETRY

Atwood, Margaret. *The Handmaid's Tale*. Boston: Houghton Mifflin, 1986.

Ballard, J. G. *Concrete Island*. New York: Vintage, 1985.

Ballard, J. G. *High Rise*. London: Jonathan Cape, 1975.

Ballard, J. G. *Super Cannes*. London: Picador, 2002.

Bellow, Saul. *Herzog. New York*. Viking Press, 1964.

Bienek, Horst. *The Cell*. Santa Barbara, Calif.: Unicorn Press, 1972.

Borges, Jorge Luis. "The Library of Babel." Trans. James E. Irby. In *Labyrinths: Selected Stories and Other Writings*, ed. Donald A. Yates and James E. Irby. New York: Modern Library, 1983.

Bradbury, Ray. *Fahrenheit 451*. New York: Barnes and Noble, 1983.

Carver, Raymond. "Cathedral." In *Cathedral*. New York: Vintage, 1983.

Cheever, John. "The Swimmer." In *Collected Short Stories of John Cheever*. New York: Random House, 1981.

Desai, Anita. "Pigeons at Daybreak." In Barbara H. Solomon, ed., *Other Voices, Other Vistas*. New York: Mentor, 1992.

Eliot, T. S. "Four Quartets." In *The Complete Poems and Plays*. London: Faber and Faber, 2004.

Eliot, T. S. "The Wasteland." In *The Complete Poems and Plays 1909–1950*. New York: Harcourt, Brace and World, 1971.

Harris, Robert. *Fatherland*. London: Hutchinson Press, 1992.

Hugo, Victor. *The Hunchback of Notre Dame*. New York: Bantam Classics, 1981.

Kafka, Franz. *Amerika*. Trans. Michael Hoffman. New York: New Directions, 2002.

Kafka, Franz. "The Burrow." In *The Complete Stories*, trans. Willa and Edwin Muir. New York: Schocken Books, 1971.

Kafka, Franz. *The Castle*. Trans. Mark Harmon. New York: Schocken Books, 1998.

Kafka, Franz. "The Great Wall of China." In *The Complete Stories*, trans. Willa and Edwin Muir. New York: Schocken Books, 1971.

Kafka, Franz. *The Trial*. Trans. Willa Muir and Edwin Muir. New York: Vintage Books, 1969.

Kafka, Franz. "Two Introductory Parables." In *The Complete Stories*, trans. Willa and Edwin Muir. New York: Schocken Books, 1971.

Koestler, Arthur. *Darkness at Noon*. New York: Bantam Books, 1966.

Mallarmé, Stéphane. *Igitur*. Paris: Gallimard, 1925.

Mallarmé, Stéphane. *Poems*. Trans. C. F. MacIntyre. Berkeley: University of California Press, 1971.

Melville, Herman. *Moby-Dick*. London:J. M. Dent and Sons, 1977.

Morley, John David. *In the Labyrinth*. London: Abacus, 1987.

Schneider, Peter. *The Wall Jumper*. New York: Pantheon Books, 1983.

Thornton, Lawrence. *Imagining Argentina*. New York: Doubleday, 1987.

Updike, John. *Rabbit Redux*. New York: Alfred A. Knopf, 1971.

Valéry, Paul. *Amphion*. In *Plays*, trans. David Paul and Robert Fitzgerald, vol. 3 of *The Collected Works of Paul Valéry*. New York: Pantheon, 1960.

Valéry, Paul. "Eupalinos, or the Architect." In *Dialogues*, trans. William McCausland Stewart, vol. 4 of *The Collected Works of Paul Valéry*. New York: Pantheon Books, 1956.

Wetherell, W. D. "The Man Who Loved Levittown." In *The Man Who Loved Levittown*. New York: Avon Books, 1985.

NONFICTION

Agamben, Giorgio. *Homo Sacer: Sovereign Power and Bare Life*. Trans. Daniel Heller-Roazen. Stanford: Stanford University Press, 1998.

Agamben, Giorgio. *State of Exception*. Trans. Kevin Attell. Chicago: University of Chicago Press, 2003.

Agamben, Giorgio. "What Is an Apparatus?" In *What Is an Apparatus? and Other Essays*, trans. David Kishik and Stefan Pedatella. Stanford: Stanford University Press, 2009.

Althusser, Louis. "Lenin and Philosophy." In *Lenin and Philosophy and Other Essays*. Trans. Ben Brewster. London: Monthly Review Press, 1971.

Arendt, Hannah. *The Human Condition*. New York: Doubleday, 1959.

Arendt, Hannah. *The Origins of Totalitarianism*. New York: Harcourt Brace Jovanovich, 1979.

Ballard, J. G. "A Handful of Dust." *Guardian*, March 20, 2006.

Barthes, Roland. "The Death of the Author." In *Image, Music, Text*, trans. Stephen Heath. New York: Hill and Wang, 1977.

Benjamin, Walter. *The Arcades Project*. Trans. Howard Eiland and Kevin McLaughlin. Cambridge: Belknap Press of Harvard University Press, 1999.

Benjamin, Walter. *Berlin Childhood Around 1900*. Trans. Howard Eiland. Cambridge: Belknap Press of Harvard University, 2006.

Benjamin, Walter. "The Destructive Character." In *Reflections: Essays, Aphorisms, Autobiographical Writings*, ed. Peter Demetz, trans. Edmund Jephcott. New York: Harcourt Brace Jovanovich, 1978.

Benjamin, Walter. "Franz Kafka." In Illuminations, ed. Hannah Arendt, trans. Harry Zohn. New York: Schocken Books, 1969.

Benjamin, Walter. "Naples." In *Reflections*, ed. Peter Demetz, trans. Edmund Jephcott. New York: Harcourt Brace Jovanovich, 1978.

Benjamin, Walter. "On the Critique of Violence." In *One-Way Street and Other Writings, trans. J. A. Underwood*. London: Penguin, 2008.

Benjamin, Walter. "Some Reflections on Kafka." In *Illuminations*, ed. Hannah Arendt, trans. Harry Zohn. New York: Schocken Books, 1969.

Berger, John. "Field." In *About Looking*. New York: Pantheon Books, 1980.

Berger, John. "Ralph Fasanella and the Experience of the City." In *About Looking*. New York: Pantheon Books, 1980.

Blanchot, Maurice. *The Space of Literature*. Trans. Ann Smock. Lincoln: University of Nebraska Press, 1982.

Bloomer, Jennifer. *Architecture and the Text: The (s)crypts of Joyce and Piranesi*. New Haven: Yale University Press, 1992.

Borges, Jorge Luis. "Herman Melville, Bartleby the Scrivner." Trans. Susanne Jill Levine. In *Selected Non-Fictions*. London: Penguin, 1999.

Borges, Jorge Luis. "Kafka and His Precursors." Trans. James E. Irby. In *Labyrinths: Selected Stories and Other Writings*, ed. Donald A. Yates and James E. Irby. New York: Modern Library, 1983.

Burgin, Richard. *Conversations with Jorge Luis Borges*. New York: Avon Books, 1968.

Calvino, Italo. *Six Memos for the Next Millennium*. Trans. Patrick Creagh. Cambridge: Harvard University Press, 1988.

Camus, Albert. "Hope and the Absurd in the Work of Franz Kafka." In *The Myth of Sisyphus and Other Essays*. New York: Alfred A. Knopf, 1955.

Canetti, Elias. *Crowds and Power. Trans. Carol Stewart*. New York: Farrar Straus Giroux, 1984.

Careri, Francesco. *Walkscapes: Walking as an Aesthetic Practice*. Barcelona: Gustavo Gili, 2003.

Colomina, Beatriz. "The Split Wall: Domestic Voyeurism." In *Sexuality and Space*, ed. Beatriz Colomina. New York: Princeton Architectural Press, 1992.

Couturier, Lisa. "Heirloom." In *The Hope of Snakes*. Boston: Beacon Press, 2005.

Davenport, Guy. "The Geography of the Imagination." In *The Geography of the Imagination*. San Francisco: North Point Press, 1981.

Davenport, Guy. "Making It Uglier to the Airport." In *Every Force Evolves a Form*. San Francisco: North Point Press, 1987.

Debord, Guy. *Situationist International Anthology*. Berkeley: Bureau of Public Secrets, 1995.

De Certeau, Michel. *The Practice of Everyday Life*. Trans. Steven Rendall. Berkeley: University of California Press, 1988.

Deleuze, Gilles. *The Fold: Leibnitz and the Baroque*. Trans. Tom Conley. Minneapolis: University of Minnesota Press, 1993.

Deleuze, Gilles. *Foucault*. Trans. Seán Hand. Minneapolis: University of Minnesota Press, 1988.

Deleuze, Gilles. "On Stuttering." In *Gilles Deleuze and the Theater of Philosophy*, ed. Constantin Boundas and Dorothea Olkowski. London: Routledge, 1996.

Deleuze, Gilles, and Félix Guattari. *Kafka: Toward a Minor Literature*. Minneapolis: University of Minnesota Press, 1992.

Deleuze, Gilles, and Félix Guattari. *A Thousand Plateaus: Capitalism and Schizophrenia*. Trans. Brian Massumi. Minneapolis: University of Minnesota Press, 1987.

Didion, Joan. "Many Mansions." In *The White Album*. New York: Washington Square Press, 1979.

Dillard, Annie. *Living by Fiction*. New York: Harper Colophon, 1982.

Eco, Umberto. *Postscript to the Name of the Rose*. Trans. William Weaver. San Diego: Harcourt Brace Jovanovich, 1983.

Forty, Adrian. *Words and Buildings: A Vocabulary of Modern Architecture*. London: Thames and Hudson, 2000.

Foucault, Michel. *Discipline and Punish: The Birth of the Prison*. Trans. Alan Sheridan. New York: Vintage-Random House, 1979.

Foucault, Michel. *Power/Knowledge: Selected Interviews and Other Writings, 1972–1977*. Ed. Colin Gordon. New York: Pantheon Books, 1980.

Frank, Ellen Eve. *Literary Architecture: Essays toward a Tradition; Walter Pater, Gerard Manley Hopkins, Marcel Proust, Henry James*. Berkeley: University of California Press, 1979.

Guattari, Félix. *Soft Subversions*. Ed. Sylvère Lotringer, trans. David L. Sweet and Chet Wiener. New York: Semiotext(e), 1996.

Hollier, Denis. *Against Architecture*. Cambridge: MIT Press, 1992.

Jameson, Fredric. *Postmodernism, or, the Cultural Logic of Late Capitalism*. Durham: Duke University Press, 1991.

Jencks, Charles. *The Language of Post-Modern Architecture*. New York: Rizzoli, 1991.

Kafka, Franz. *The Blue Octavo Notebooks*. Trans. Ernst Kaiser and Eithne Wilkins. Cambridge: Exact Change, 1991.

Klee, Paul. *On Modern Art*. London: Faber and Faber, 1948.

Klee, Paul. *Pedagogical Sketchbook*. New York: Nierendorf Gallery, 1944.

Koyré, Alexandre. *From the Closed World to the Infinite Universe*. Baltimore: Johns Hopkins University Press, 1968.

Corbusier, Le. *When the Cathedrals Were White: A Journey to the Country of Timid People*. Trans. Francis Hyslop. London: Routledge, 1947.

Lefebvre, Henri. *The Production of Space*. Trans. Donald Nicholson-Smith. Oxford: Blackwell, 1991.

Lefebvre, Henri. "Reflections on the Politics of Space." *Antipode Journal* 8 (2) (1976): 33.

Lowenthal, Leo. *An Unmastered Past*. Ed. Martin Jay. Berkeley: University of California Press, 1987.

Lukács, Georg. *History and Class Consciousness*. Trans. Rodney Livingstone. Merlin Press, 1967.

Mallarmé, Stéphane. "Crise de vers." In *Oeuvres complètes*. Paris: Gallimard, 1945.

Marx, Karl. *The Marx Engels Reader*. New York: W. W. Norton, 1978.

McEwen, Indra Kagis. *Socrates' Ancestor*. Cambridge: MIT Press, 1994.

Meed, Vladka. *On Both Sides of the Wall*. Trans. Steven Meed. New York: Holocaust Library, 1979.

Nietzsche, Friedrich. *The Gay Science*. Ed. Bernard Williams. Cambridge: Cambridge University Press, 2001.

Rice, Charles. *The Emergence of the Interior*. London: Routledge, 2007.

Ringelblum, Emmanuel. *Notes from the Warsaw Ghetto: Journal of Emmanuel Ringelblum*. Trans. and ed. Jacob Sloane. New York: Schocken Books, 1974.

Robbe-Gillet, Alain. *For a New Novel: Essays on Fiction*. Trans. Richard Howard. New York: Grove Press, 1965.

Rowe, Colin, and Robert Slutzky. "Transparency: Literal and Phenomenal." In Colin Rowe, *The Mathematics of the Ideal Villa and Other Essays*. Cambridge: MIT Press, 1973.

Schmitt, Carl. *The Concept of the Political*. Chicago: University of Chicago Press, 1996.

Schneider, Peter. "If the Wall Came Tumbling Down." Trans. Krishna Winston. *New York Times*, June 1989, 25.

Segrest, Robert, and Jennifer Bloomer. "Without Architecture." Special issue, *Art Papers* 8, no. 4 (1984).

Stoner, Jill. "Camp and Field: Notes on the Polish Landscape." *Traditional Dwellings and Settlements Review* 3, no. 1 (1991).

Stoner, Jill. "The Falcon's Return." *Places* 12, no. 3 (1999).

Stoner, Jill. *Poems for Architects*. San Francisco: William Stout Publishers, 2001.

Struik, Derek. *A Concise History of Mathematics*. New York: Dover, 1948.

Strumiłło, Władysław. "Environmental Means of Control and Resistance: Case Study Warsaw." Unpublished paper, 1980.

Tafuri, Manfredo. *Architecture and Utopia: Design and Capitalist Development*. Trans. Barbara Luigia Le Penta. Cambridge: MIT Press, 1976.

Thomas, Lewis. "The Attic of the Brain." In *Late Night Thoughts on Listening to Mahler's Ninth Symphony*. New York: Penguin, 1995.

Timerman, Jacobo. *Prisoner Without a Name, Cell Without a Number.* Trans. Toby Talbot, introduction by Arthur Miller. Madison: University of Wisconsin Press, 2002.

Valéry, Paul. *Introduction to the Method of Leonardo da Vinci.* Trans. Thomas McGreevy. London: John Rodker, 1929.

Vargish, Thomas, and Delo E. Mook. *Inside Modernism: Relativity Theory, Cubism, Narrative.* New Haven: Yale University Press, 1999.

Virilio, Paul. "A Glimpse." In *A Landscape of Events.* Cambridge: MIT Press, 2000.

White, E. B. *Here Is New York.* New York: Harper, 1949.

Woolf, Virginia. *The Collected Essays.* London: Hogarth Press, 1966.

Woolf, Virginia. *A Room of One's Own.* Orlando: Harcourt, 2005.

ETYMOLOGY REFERENCES

Claiborne, Robert. *The Roots of English.* New York: Times Books, 1989.

Watkins, Calvin, ed. *The American Heritage Dictionary of Indo-European Roots.* Boston: Houghton Mifflin, 1985.

Cubism, 48, 131

Daedalus, 41–42, 128, 151

Davenport, Guy, 116, 128, 141

Da Vinci, Leonardo, 42, 66

Debord, Guy, 113

De Certeau, Michel, 16, 116

Deleuze, Gilles, 1, 3, 7, 13, 18, 32, 54, 61, 64, 67, 68, 76, 89, 95, 104, 110, 111, 114, 117, 118, 121, 124, 132, 133, 146, 152

De Quincey, Thomas, 129

Desai, Anita, 99, 152

Detroit, 101

Didion, Joan, 139

Dillard, Annie, 115, 153

Dirty War (Argentina), 30, 123, 146

Docklands, 73

Eco, Umberto, 128

Eddington, Arthur, 26, 119

Einstein, Albert, 48, 64

Eliot, T. S., 49, 60, 131, 140

Eupalinos, 72, 91, 151

Evans, Robin, 123

Faraday, Michael, 123

Fascism, 117

Fassanella, Ralph, 126

Fiorentino, Mario, 85